T0271106

Market Distortions in Privatisation Processes

Drawing on a range of global case studies, *Market Distortions in Privatisation Processes* illustrates the ways in which market distortions damaged the ability of privatisation processes to yield concrete benefits to consumers.

The book compares and contrasts privatisations of state-owned enterprises around the world where competition informed the regulatory design and thus liberated consumer welfare. In particular, the cases are drawn from the electricity and gas sector, the telecoms industry, and postal services—each of which has been frequently privatised in different context. For each industry, the book explores the UK and US experiences as well as looking at international cases from both developed and developing countries, including, where appropriate, Japan, Colombia, Romania and Mexico. The emphasis is on analysing the impact that market distortions have had on the outcomes of those privatisations. The book also looks at how public service objectives were achieved and how they too can be designed in pro-competitive or anti-competitive ways.

This book will be of significant interest to readers in international business, economics and law.

Shanker Singham is one of the world's leading international trade and competition lawyer and economists. He is a former advisor to both the UK Secretary of State for International Trade (2016–2018) as well as a former cleared advisor to the United States Trade Representative (2009–2016). He has led the market access and WTO practices of two large global law firms, and has advised governments and multinationals. He is author of *A General Theory of Trade and Competition: Trade Liberalisation and Competitive Markets* (CMP, 2007) and over 100 book chapters and articles. He is the lead author of the Singham-Rangan-Bradley model to measure Anti-Competitive Market Distortions.

Market Distortions in Privatisation Processes

Shanker Singham

Routledge
Taylor & Francis Group

LONDON AND NEW YORK

First published 2023
by Routledge
4 Park Square, Milton Park, Abingdon, Oxon OX14 4RN

and by Routledge
605 Third Avenue, New York, NY 10158

Routledge is an imprint of the Taylor & Francis Group, an informa business

British Library Cataloguing-in-Publication Data
A catalogue record for this book is available from the British Library

ISBN: 978-1-032-41935-0 (hbk)
ISBN: 978-1-032-41936-7 (pbk)
ISBN: 978-1-003-36047-6 (ebk)

DOI: 10.4324/9781003360476

Typeset in Times New Roman
by Apex CoVantage, LLC

Contents

1 Impact of Market Distortions in the Specific Case of Privatisation

This volume analyses the impact of market distortions in the specific case of privatisation. Many of the distortions which are set out in the Normative Framework for Anti-Competitive Market Distortions are in full view in the case of privatisations. There has also now been a significant history or privatisations all over the world and so it is useful to analyse a number of these in order to understand which have been successful, which have not been, and what lessons can be drawn.

The Privatisation Conundrum

Privatisation simply means the introduction into private hands of certain means of production, which had historically been controlled by the state. This can be affected in a number of ways:

1 The State can sell its assets to private providers.
2 The State can contract out its services to private vendors.
3 The State can progressively deregulate to allow private competitors to compete.
4 The State could give privileges to a private vendor to provide a service in a specific area, protected by a legislative monopoly.

There are many other ways that the private sector and public sector can work together, but we confine our definitions of privatisation to the aforementioned examples. Other kinds of so-called privatisation, such as corporatisation, hardly count given the fact that they frequently merely convert public monopoly with regulation to private monopoly without regulation.

The World Bank[1] and a number of commentators have done studies about the privatisations which took place in the 1990s and concluded that there are a certain number of key elements that are required with respect to

DOI: 10.4324/9781003360476-1

privatisation. Drawing on that experience, we highlight key principles for success.

1   Privatisation works best if it is part of a larger programme of reforms promoting efficiency and competitive markets.
2   Regulation is critical to the successful privatisation of monopolies.
3   Privatisation must be accompanied by competition.
4   Setting up a privatisation for a competitive outcome is critical.[2]

Privatisation on its own will not necessarily be the cure for underperforming state-owned enterprises (SOEs), but rather, if done properly and in a way that liberates the forces of competition, will lead ultimately to benefits for the economy. It is clear that one must avoid a situation all too common in the 90s, which was the conversion of public monopoly with regulation to private monopoly without regulation. The result visits potential harm on consumers. While there is broad agreement that the private sector should own the means of production of goods and services in general, there is a difference of opinion when it comes to public goods or, more accurately, goods that display public goods characteristics (for closer analysis of public goods, see the chapter on media). Those who set a high value on competition conclude that privatisation is best even here, in particular in those public goods sectors (such as in the media sector) where markets can be broadened dramatically due to technology.

Here, monopolistic competition (where different platforms carry content to very large markets) means that private ownership of public goods can deliver economic benefits and can even achieve the social goals for which regulation was thought to be required. In other words, there are public goods cases where market failure is not reached (because the market can be expanded dramatically) or is reached much later than public goods theory would ordinarily predict.

In its analysis of Asian privatisation, the Asian Development Bank (ADB) has highlighted a number of key points in its Special Evaluation Study on the Privatisation of Public Sector Enterprises: Lessons for Developing Member Countries, December 2001.[3] These points include the fact that too many countries focus on regulation when their real aim should be increasing competition as a result of the privatisation. In particular, sequencing that delays the introduction of competition after privatisation or rations it by limiting entry lessens the benefits of privatisation. Privatisation with competition benefits consumers, because of reduction in prices and improvement in services. More troublesome and linked to the points made above regarding the benefits of liberalisation in overly regulated markets, a lack of competition may even lead to a contraction of benefits to consumers and the economy.

The ADB study has shown that there are a number of key benefits as a result of privatisation:

1   Provision of budgetary relief, where SOEs operate in inefficient ways largely because persistent SOE losses will be curtailed.
2   Increasing international standing, and increased efficiency in management.
3   Increased foreign investment through increasing foreign investor confidence, increased efficiency in management, and attract foreign technology.
4   Increased efficiency in management and the economy will lead to a more developed domestic capital market, and a broader ownership base of public assets.

However, given the powerful political interests at play, transparency and competitive bidding are key elements in securing a successful privatisation.

In most studies the need for careful sequencing is of paramount importance. The ADB study in particular notes that there is a "preoccupation with regulation without first considering the scope for competition and how to increase it to minimise regulation."[4]

The ADB notes the usefulness of the competition authority in ensuring that the regulator does not demonstrate capture weaknesses and also to ensure a pro-competitive regulatory environment.

Hence, we can see that competition agencies can play a critical role in ensuring that the benefits of privatisation for consumers can be realised. This is because these groups are the main bulwark against the powerful political forces which would otherwise capture the privatisation process and reap its monopoly rents. We will discuss their role in greater detail in Chapter 3.

Privatisations are often brought about by a number of external factors, including the need for foreign investment, the need to make state-run companies more efficient and the need for hard currency. However, in many cases, privatisations do not succeed in liberating value to consumers because the initial sale is not accompanied by the kind of pro-competitive regulation that leads to consumer empowerment. In many cases, in countries that are transitioning out of some form of state control or governmental intervention in the economy, the lack of pro-competitive regulation arises because the institutions that underpin such pro-competitive regulations are not strong enough to withstand the winds of political pressure, in particular the pressure exerted by the newly privatised entity which is usually a politically powerful incumbent company. In some cases, the relevant competition laws do not exist, or other administrative remedies are used to subvert the economic purposes of the competition law. In these cases, the benefits of competition policy and pro-competitive regulation are lost. Ultimately this is a broader issue of the playing out of producer interests versus consumer interests, of competition policy versus industrial policy. On the basis of the principles set forth earlier, we will review the kinds of policies and regulations that prevent the consumer welfare enhancing effects of privatisation to be unleashed. We will look in detail at the following types of practices that might adversely distort markets in the privatisation context:

1   Uncompetitive rules on interconnection in telecommunications.
2   Cross subsidisation in a number of services sectors.
3   State aids.
4   Uncompetitive price regulation.
5   Allowing competitor producer welfare concerns to trump consumer welfare concerns in the regulatory framework and also the application of competition law.

We will examine these issues in detail in subsequent chapters, but the general themes can be developed by understanding the issues that prevented liberalisation from being as good for consumers as had been initially hoped. In the 1980s and 1990s, there were many privatisations responding to global liberalisation processes where such failures can be observed. Many of them were in developing countries. We see some additional common themes from these failures.

6   Not properly accounting for investment requirements, and then allowing political concerns to trump economic ones (Dominican Republic electricity privatisation).
7   Allowing some sectors to remain closed while others are exposed to competition, and then ensuring that anti-competitive harms do not spill over (California Electricity, Mexico telecoms).
8   Allowing state aids to continue in newly privatised industries (China SOEs).
9   Allowing monopolisation of an essential facility (Mexico telecoms).

Public Versus Private Ownership: The Real Issue

Contrary to conventional wisdom, the issue of ownership is not always the most important issue in determining the overall impact of the government on the productive process. Sappington and Stiglitz have argued that the real issue is the transaction cost that the government faces when attempting to intervene "in delegated production activities. Government intervention is generally less costly under public ownership, but a promise not to intervene is more credible under private production, and it can also have beneficial incentive effects."[5]

The real issue is what impact government intervention has on the market. Clearly in an SOE the damage caused by government intervention is high, but it is not absent merely because an entity is private. In the case of an SOE, both the motivation and identity of the Government affect how government decisions impact the productive process. Unfortunately, governments tend to be revenue and not profit maximisers (and sometimes not even that). Managers may therefore pursue objectives other than the ones that a profit-maximising rival might pursue. The fact that SOEs cannot go bankrupt or can be saved from bankruptcy by their owner governments also dramatically affects their behaviour, since they can engage in loss-making activity for much longer than their private rivals typically can. This fundamentally changes the risk/reward calculus which is at the heart of the free market system.

As has been mentioned, private ownership of property generally leads to better utilisation of that property. Hence, by analogy, state-owned companies experience a sudden improvement in their management systems after a privatisation are able to focus on business efficiency and improvement, without having to consider other political goals which may be foisted on them by the ministries that either control them or to whom they are responsible. However, while no doubt increased efficiency is a major benefit of privatisation, the most important improvement is that without the monopoly, consumer welfare will be enhanced as there will be greater levels of competition. However, consumers are frequently far from a privatising government's mind, when the regulations accompanying privatisation are crafted. In order to understand how these different arguments play out in the political context, it is useful to look at the lead-up and history surrounding some of these issues in the context of the UK privatisation programme of the 1980s, which was one of the first series of privatisations.

History of Privatisation in Britain

With the exception of certain privatisations in Chile, many of the last four decades' privatisations began in Britain. In order to understand the privatisation process in Britain, it is necessary to look back at the approach that Britain has had to private property throughout the end of the 19th century and subsequently. The concept of private property has historically been very strong. John Locke had first postulated the notion that individual property rights were natural rights which were not conferred on individuals by their governments but were rather recognised by governments. Britain as a free trade nation following the corn law repeal (see earlier) had embraced laissez-faire economics and Adam Smith. It had been widely accepted in Britain that profits should be controlled by the market and not through government regulation. Shortly after the Second World War, the sanctity of the property right was brought into question by the Attlee government which had been returned with a landslide in 1945 at the end of the War. People questioned high profits from the standpoint of an equitable distribution of resources (much as some in the UK and the US do now). However, because Britain lacked meaningful disciplines that prevented anti-competitive conduct, some of these high profits could be attributed to anti-competitive practices or cartels. This became one of the arguments for nationalisation, which was problematic because similar results could have been achieved through sound antitrust enforcement.

The rise of the Labour Party in Britain in the early part of the 20th century, and the General Strike of 1926, had laid the foundations for nationalisation as a way of shifting wealth from rich entrepreneurs to poor people. Public ownership of the means of production, at least for certain kinds of utilities that we now describe as network utilities began to gain widespread acceptance as people felt that private companies pursued private profit to their detriment. During this period, largely because public ownership was deemed to be pro-poor, it was often the default policy choice, often without an actual analysis of the facts. Indeed, during the 1960s and 1970s in many countries the World Bank and other International Financial Institutions paid large amounts to state-owned utility companies. These payments were not always used in profit-maximising ways and might have led to continued inefficiencies and a forestalling of the proper development of the private sector. However, as the macro-economic performance of the SOEs declined, there was a revision in the minds of economists as to whether SOEs were indeed the most optimal way of managing utilities. The performance of these enterprises was almost always weak.[6]

When the British government embarked on a whole scale programme of privatisation under the leadership of Margaret Thatcher, it did so for many reasons. The reason given by Margaret Thatcher in her memoirs, The Downing Street Years,[7] was that successive labour (and conservative) governments had gradually ratcheted Britain more and more towards accepting socialism. Britain openly embraced socialism, statism and government intervention. It was the intention of the Thatcher government to return Britain to the straight and narrow path of free markets and getting government out of the economy. It is likely that Thatcher also saw the privatisation of the larger public utilities as a way of breaking the power of big labour which had strangled the British economy in the 1970s and ultimately led to the fall of the previous government. It was the desire not to be held to ransom by big labour that made the government focus on energy (privatisation of the National Coal Board, and consequent electricity privatisation), and steel (together, the traditional bastions of labour power). The 1983 Conservative manifesto declared that the following previously state owned or controlled companies would be privatised, Rolls Royce, British Airways, British Steel, British Shipbuilders, British Leyland as well as Britain's airports. This was a monumental task. According to the manifesto, the purpose of this was to "expose [state-owned companies] to real competition." To announce the list was a gauntlet thrown down in the face of the British trade union movement, and those who still believed that public ownership was a valid policy choice.

One interesting development which did not necessarily apply to some of the other privatisations that took place in the 1990s was that Britain's economic performance in the decade before the Thatcher government was so poor. The great enemy during the 1970s was inflation, and the need to ensure that counter-inflationary policy elements were included in the privatisation process itself meant that there was some downward pressure on the sales prices of the public utilities themselves. This ensured that investors would not overpay, but it also had an impact on the investment capabilities of new buyers. There then followed privatisation of some of the network utilities where the reasons behind the privatisation were less clear because we were then dealing with products and services to which public goods theories applied.

Clearly if the market replaced the State, regulators had to give some thought to how competition might operate in a system that had hitherto been a state-owned system with no competition. As has been stated, these developments resulted from the desire to turn back the clock from the state's involvement in these sectors. Broadly, there were three ways that were tried to ensure that in the case of countrywide networks, the benefits of market competition did not mean that scale efficiencies were lost. These three methods involved some degree of state control ranged from central state ownership, allowing companies to gain dominant status through a relaxed antitrust policy allowing mergers and consolidation, or monopolistic competition, where multiple platforms competed against each other.

The US Experience

In the US, privatisation processes meant that most utilities were sold with a contractual franchise which gave exclusivity for a fixed duration. Some of these contractual franchises were for 50 years. In the case of the telephony system, the expiration of the Bell patents, led to new entry and lower prices. As has proved to be common in these cases, Bell then tried to preserve its position by engaging in anti-competitive interconnection policy. This was a typical incumbent's response to new entry, and we will see it repeatedly in the examples that we discuss in detail. Political lobbying was relied on to protect Bell's position. Bell remained successful even after the expiry of its patents, because it then acquired a number of companies and became the market leader for provision of mass market telephony. In the case of electricity, the early providers of power in the US were private companies (at the beginning of the 20th century, e.g., only a small percentage (less than 10%) of electrical utilities were public).[8] The Great Depression changed the pattern of regulation and moved the US towards state level regulation, through the Public Utilities Holding Company Act of 1935, and the Natural Gas Act of 1938. The unintended consequence of this was to ensure that the state-level companies were insulated from competition. However, it is important to understand that the background to the provision of utility services in the US was the regulation of private companies.

Both the US and the UK history illustrate the fundamental tension between investors and consumers in the privatisation process. The regulatory design must balance these interests, but it will be vital for consumer welfare enhancement to play a significant role to offset producer bias. The key issue will depend on the results of a non-cooperative game between regulator and regulated. It will also depend on how well the notion of consumer welfare enhancement is actually advanced in the regulatory process. While the notion of benefits to the regulated entity in exchange for investment in facility and plant is well understood, the notion of consumer welfare enhancement in the regulatory process is much less understood and applied.

In general, regulatory agencies tend not to factor into their regulatory considerations consumer welfare enhancement concerns. The regulatory focus is usual to ensure other objectives such as revenue maximisation, job creation and other social goals.

The various methods of regulating network utilities illustrate how the game between regulator and regulatee can work. In the US, the prevalent type of regulation is rate of return regulation. Rate of return regulation is regulation where prices are set at average, rather than marginal cost. The purpose of this is to ensure that utilities charge at prices that allow them to recoup their costs with a profit. However, the problem here is that there is little incentive to cut costs and therefore increase efficiency. In the compact between regulator and regulated, problems can arise if consumer welfare is ignored or made subservient to the needs of the incumbent producer. The political power of the incumbent can lead to consumer damage. The question is precisely what type of regulation is being applied and how it can be used to favour either an incumbent producer or consumer interest. We will examine this in detail in later chapters which focus on particular industry sectors. An important point to bear in mind in this discussion is the fact that frequently these regulated industries represent a substantial input cost for other important industries (e.g., energy costs amount to 15% of the price of steel, although some estimates are considerably higher).[9]

In developing country markets, the institutions that underpinned privatisation such as competition agencies and regulators in the US and the UK were (and are) far less developed. This lack of institutional strength had important consequences for the privatisations there. The record on privatisations in Central and Eastern Europe closely followed the transition from Soviet domination and is instructive. In the case of these countries, privatisation of the different utilities occurred at different times and for different reasons. In particular privatisation of electricity has caused problems because in many developing countries, consumers had been paying very little for these services, either because of large-scale governmental programmes or in many cases because of piracy. The notion that electricity (or indeed water) is something that must be paid for is alien to many people in countries where theft of electricity is normal. This creates great tension in the context of the regulatory compact between regulator and regulated entity that we discussed earlier. Indeed, this consumer pressure, even though it is "consumer pressure" of a very different nature to the notion of consumer welfare that is a general theme of this book, can lead to regulatory failure. In this context, it is important that regulators and government ministers fully understand what "consumer" means in the economic context. "Consumer welfare" is much misunderstood concept. Policy and rule-makers must understand that consumer welfare enhancement does not simply mean lower prices or more competition for its own sake. It refers to the precise nature of the relevant supply and demand curves and how the consumer welfare enhancing market equilibrium can be reached and preserved. This equilibrium maximises both productive and allocative efficiency and minimises deadweight losses to consumers.

It also is very relevant to ask the question what credible pressure can be applied to the host country in the event that there is a regulatory failure. If the regulatory breakdown is a violation of WTO rules or other multilateral or regional rules to which the host country is a party, this is grounds for WTO claim against the country and consequent trade sanctions. Increasingly certain services are within the GATS framework, and we will see how this plays out in a number of different areas. In addition, non-compliance with WTO obligations brings into play a range of issues that impact other areas of leverage, such as the Generalised System of Preferences or even aid-related issues such as the Millennium Challenge Account goals.[10]

As we look at specific cases, we note that there is a spectrum of privatisation. Different sectors lend themselves to privatisation and competitive markets in different ways. For example, in the case of airline privatisation, the arguments in favour of state ownership or regulation are slight. While the sunk capital costs are not insignificant, they are not at the level of what is required to build out an electricity system or a telecoms network for example. In these latter cases, there is an argument, based on public goods theory and natural monopoly theory which is a stronger argument in favour of public ownership and more intrusive regulation. However, we will demonstrate that even in these sectors the benefits of competition and functioning markets usually outweigh the costs, and that, there are significant unintended consequences where the state continues to control these sectors or to interfere in them economically.

Telecoms Industry

Most telecoms privatisations involve a trade-off between competition principles and the need to give the investor appropriate incentives. The way this trade-off is generally resolved is by giving the concessionaire a limited monopoly for a fixed period. After the expiration of that period, gradual liberalisation normally takes place, usually by maintaining a monopoly over local service, while simultaneously opening up long distance and international service to new entrants. What ordinarily follows is a process of rate rebalancing. Under this mechanism, local rates that were historically very low must be increased, while long distance and international rates which were historically very high must be rebalanced to ensure that they approach competitive levels. We will first review some examples of privatisations in countries and then make some general comments about how they have worked. We will also focus on the Mexican privatisation and its aftermath as this is one of the first demonstrations of the violation of WTO principles as well as domestic competition law, which went through full WTO dispute resolution.

Many of the Central and Eastern European countries have privatised their telecoms industries. In the case of the Czech Republic, the privatisation of the telecoms industry was both a de-monopolisation and a liberalisation. The Czech privatisation was unusual because it preserved a monopoly over long distance voice telephony. A small number of operators did get licenses to enter the local market. The problem here was the sequencing of the liberalisation. The incumbent Czech operator, STP Telecom was able to maintain its market dominance. The fact that it also owned the cellular phone service further compounded its market dominance. The question then becomes whether the Czech institutions which are designed to limit anti-competitive behaviour could be successful in reining in the incumbent's behaviour. In most experiences they have not been successful in doing this in part because of the power of the incumbent and in part because of the weakness of the competition agencies themselves. We have seen similar problems which plagued the Polish privatisation, which also arose from the precise sequencing of how the market is opened. As in the Czech process, in Poland the monopoly was preserved in long distance. Unsurprisingly the incumbent company's market share was hardly changed even several years after the privatisation.

In the UK, telecoms privatisation was followed by a duopoly policy. This policy was criticised as stunting the ability of the privatisation to truly unleash the forces of competition. The privatisation brought to the fore the manner in which price regulation was conducted. In contrast to the Chilean electricity costs where costs were attributed to a hypothetical operator, and used as a base for cost-based regulation, in the UK, a system based on the retail price index was used to build in an "acceptable" profit element. The problem with this kind of regulation is that it does not apply downward pressure to costs. In fact there were not significant increases in BT's over-all productivity in the first 6 years when this was the prevalent system of regulation. The Mexican privatisation, which we describe in detail in Chapter 14, of Teléfonos de Mexico was also conducted on the basis of RPI-X, with X set at zero in 1991–1996, then at 3%, and thereafter reset every 4 years.[11] The problem is that this regulation which gave a price cap over a basket of services set the stage for wholesale anti-competitive practices in the future which Mexico is still experiencing. Of all the privatisations, it is clear that the Chilean model is one of the only privatisations where care was actually paid to create a regulatory system focused on applying competitive pressure to lower cost and increase efficiency. Rate of return regulation which effectively puts the regulator in the shoes of the previous government determining the appropriate level of profit has been tried in numerous cases and has not led to downward pressure on costs. Indeed, that is one of the reasons that public utilities and rate of return regulated, vertically integrated franchise monopolies act in very similar ways. We will analyse the different methods of regulation to look at their impact on the competitive process and on consumer welfare.

Energy

Electricity privatisations in particular have been fraught with difficulty. In Hungary, the production of electricity was controlled by a trust between 1963 and 1992. There were two relevant entities, the State Property Agency (SPA) and the electricity companies' overall holding company. These entities had very different approaches to the liberalisation process—The SPA wanted to sell the assets quickly, whereas the holding company wanted to maintain and manage them. The restructuring of the industry between 1990 and 1992 was modelled on the UK electricity privatisation. The Hungarian privatisation illustrates one of the areas where electricity privatisation has a different impact in developing as opposed to developed markets. In developed markets the unleashed forces of competition have a downward impact on price, but in developing markets, regulators are brought under tremendous pressure from political forces to operate a price cap because the price has been artificially low because of government subsidy, or an unbalanced system where local rates are artificially reduced, and long-distance rates are increased (in the case of telecom). The operation of the cap then meant that the lowest prices were to domestic households and businesses paid higher prices (in contrast to the cost of supply). This then created a group of individual consumers who did not want to see a rebalancing of the rates to consumer welfare optimising levels. In the case of telecom, this rebalancing would lead to higher local, but lower long-distance rates. The irony is that this means that there was a vocal constituency of consumers who were actively opposing a consumer welfare optimising outcome. In reality this is often the case in these kinds of situations. There is a difference between present and future consumers. While present consumers may want lower prices now, future consumers are concerned about the efficiency of the enterprises that are producing products so that prices in the future remain at competitive levels. This tension is not always well understood by consumer advocacy groups, and this has been particularly true in the case of network industry privatisations.

In the case of many privatisations, including energy, telecoms and other privatisations, the government is besieged by concerns that the rebalancing process referred to above has in fact led to higher prices for some classes of consumer. These consumers generally complain about the increased prices, leading governments to erroneously match the interests of present consumers with the interests of future ones. Future consumers actually need the initially higher prices in certain market segments that arise from the increasing efficiency that comes from a successful liberalisation which maximises productive efficiency.

One significant difference in electricity privatisation is the role of primarily state-owned electricity companies that are actively engaged with privatisations. State-owned companies, as we will discuss at length in due course, are not profit maximisers, and hence may be able or willing to accept losses that other businesses would not accept. Hence, if they are adversely affected by the regulatory game, they may attach a lower level of interest on efficiency and profit maximisation, and this may lead to a less consumer welfare enhancing outcome.

The precise apportionment of costs is an integral part of the regulatory process. In Chile, the electricity privatisation was accompanied by cost-based regulation (as opposed to price-based regulation). This was important because cost-based regulation created an incentive to lower costs and increasing efficiency, whereas price-based regulation does not set up that incentive.

Postal Experience

Historically in most countries, postal and telecoms operators were under the same overall agency—the Post and Telecom Ministry. In the US, however, postal service was always supplied by the government but telecommunications (initially telegraphy) were provided from the outset by the private sector. Western Union was the predominant telegraphic services carrier in the 19th century. It achieved network economies by merging with rivals. In Britain, by contrast, the Post Office was created as a statutory monopoly in the 16th century. The Post Office was able to charge very low prices because of its government ownership. When telegraph companies were nationalised in Britain, they were transferred to the Post Office. While the Post Office ran telegraphy, it developed a system of cross-subsidies to enable it to do so. The Bell and Edison companies came to the UK to set up telephone exchanges in competition with the Post Office and the reaction was for the Post Office to apply to the courts for the telephone company to be determined to be operating telegraphic service that was part of the reserved sector of the Post Office monopoly. The Post Office then acted as any monopolist would with respect to the private telephone companies then present. Problems continued until the complete nationalisation in 1911. Many of these arguments are now being played out as the postal sector seeks to establish the limits of its reserved sector. What this demonstrates is that the problem was not that there was always a national state-owned company providing these services, but rather that certain populist and redistributive philosophies built the case for active nationalisation, which occurred at various points through the history of the 20th century.

De-Integration as a Way of Introducing Competition

Many network utilities were vertically integrated prior to their privatisations. The electricity industry is an example of introducing competition.

Much of the economic literature looks at privatisation of network utilities through the lens of retaining what is frequently described as a "natural monopoly" core and a competitive market in other areas. This language is potentially dangerous as it can lead to undue protection to the "core" which actually distorts the market in other non-core areas, which are subject to competition. We have seen this played out in many of the case studies we examine in more detail.

Applying game theoretical concepts helps us to understand regulatory choices by governments. Interest group regulation suggests that the beneficiaries will be on the production side of the equation—producer welfare is prioritised more highly than consumer welfare because of the political bias in favour of producers. Producer benefits are easily identified, whereas consumer benefits are diverse and diffuse. This analysis of regulation explains the surprisingly common fact of regulatory capture which we will see played out in specific case studies. The risk of capture seems to be particularly prevalent in developing countries where consumer interests are even less to the fore. The theory also lends support to the notion that ownership is not necessarily the be all and end of all of delivery of a competitive market. What matters is the quality of regulation, and whether it is moving the market to a pro-competitive or anti-competitive equilibrium. Regulatory reform usually requires some crisis or cataclysmic event to promote it.

Energy policy itself can also be a market distorter in other ways, that is, when certain types of business are given cheaper power, this distorts their cost base via their competitors and can lead to adverse competitive effects.

Market Competition as a Method of Regulation

We believe that it is generally accepted that competition is the best way to apply downward pressure to the costs base of network industries. On the other hand, cost of service regulation, or rate of return do not lead to downward pressure on costs. All other things being equal, efficiency gains therefore can best be achieved through market competition. Price cap regulation in particular leads often to the cap becoming a floor and so can have anti-competition effects. The Chilean examples that we note earlier illustrate an attempt to benchmark utilities so that the regulatory environment does impose some sort of downward pressure on costs. Perhaps one of the most significant impacts of increasing competition is that this increases the risk of failure and therefore alters the behaviour of managers.

Market competition also has the advantage that upon privatisation, there is a tendency for non-competitive forces to lead to coordination effects that serve to increase costs. Some of these effects may also lead to over-engineering, that is, where services or technologies are developed that have no real commercial use or demand. These latter effects are encouraged by rate-of-return regulation. Rate-of-return regulation also encourages inefficient ways to spend the firm's money, in terms of both research and management choices (e.g. the US Postal Service sponsoring the US cycling team).[12]

The benefits of liberalisation come with competition, and the precise method that leads to greater levels of competition will largely determine whether the privatisation has been successful or not. Historically, these coordination effects have assumed to be more important for telecoms than, say for gas and electricity. However, this does not take into account technological bypass issues, where the entire playing field changes. In other words, wireless telephony can simply act as a competitor to wire line services so that the anti-competitive effects in the wire line sector can be overcome by this alternative technology. Similarly Voice Over the Internet (VOIP) telephony can act as yet another potential entrant that limits the likelihood that coordination in the telephony sector from having adverse consequences for consumers. However, in looking at the impact of potential new technologies, one must bear in mind the ability of the incumbent to block the development of new technologies.[13] Hausman suggests that the development of mobile telephony was delayed by regulatory decisions (specifically the precise manner of the divestiture of AT&T), leading to up to $100 billion in losses for consumers.[14]

One example of the lack of impact on the competitive market was the privatisation of British Gas. The privatisation of British Gas was set up by the Gas Act, 1986. However, attempts by others to secure gas access failed until 1990, because British Gas simply foreclosed access. Finally, the UK competition agency (at the time) the Office of Fair Trading forced British Gas to open up at least 10% of gas access. The MMC had found that British Gas had been using its market power to deter entry and competition, recommending that retail competition be introduced by separating the trading arm of British Gas. The DTI stopped short of structural separation but did mandate accounting separation. There was competition in the production area, because British Gas was in competition with other countries' gas producers. However, once the gas left the beachhead, it had to flow along British Gas's pipes. The next stage in the introduction of competition was the competitive auction of storage.

In contrast to telephony and gas, in the case of electricity, the industry was restructured prior to privatisation. As such, this was a recognition that competition could best be introduced by restructuring, as opposed to merely hoping that privatisation would lead to competition (as it eventually did in the case of British Gas, in excess of a decade after the Gas Act itself).

The US Airline Deregulation

The deregulation of the US airline industry illustrates the impact that competition can have. After the Airline Deregulation Act of 1978, 49 new airlines were certified for domestic passenger service between 1979 and 1983, but there was also rapid exit for unprofitable airlines so that only 12 remained by 1992 (of which there were only 3 of the larger new entrants). Route competition did increase dramatically from 1.5 equivalent airlines in 1978 to 2.5 in 1988.[15] There was also a wholesale industry reorganisation, which eventually led to the hub and spoke model, a key element of modern air travel.

The Question of Natural Monopoly

As we have noted, many commentators assume that the core networks of utilities are natural monopolies. However, this is often assumed and not tested. Natural monopoly implies that normal market conditions somehow do not lead to consumer welfare optimising outcomes in cases where all the demand can be satisfied at the lowest cost by one firm rather than two or more. People frequently assume that this is the case for utilities or industries with very substantial sunk costs. As Richard Posner originally set out in great detail in his 1969 essay on "Natural Monopoly and Its Regulation,"[16] before one too readily assumes that the conditions are right for natural monopoly, one must be very careful about the catastrophically damaging impact that monopoly, natural or otherwise, has on price, efficiency, and technological advancement. One must be mindful that industries that are prone to the natural monopoly label are those that are frequently on the cutting edge of technological development and so the effect of monopoly on innovation must be carefully weighed, especially in light of available alternatives. We must also differentiate between a private monopoly arrived at through ordinary competitive forces and a government-granted monopoly.

The problem with the natural monopoly approach is where it leads. Even if the competitive business and non-competitive natural monopoly can be separated out, which is not easy, they nevertheless interact with one another, and merely preserving the non-competitive core can set up the conditions for anti-competitive behaviour in the future.

Physical differences also have an impact. In the case of electricity, it cannot be stored, and fails to safety. Gas can be stored but fails to danger. In both cases, electrons and gas molecules are the same, so there does not need to be a direct link between producers and consumers. In the case of telephony, there does. In the former case, one can have pools to create competitive conditions. In telephony, this is not possible, because each transaction is a personal one. All of these complexities must be understood by the regulator and competition agency.

State Ownership of Utilities

A question that we will examine in greater detail is whether it is possible to introduce pro-competitive reforms, while still maintaining state ownership over the utility. The problem is usually that with state ownership come a range of benefits that do not flow to private sector companies. Some of these benefits include special tax treatment, special treatment in customs (postal companies), and the preservation of mandated monopolies in certain core areas (see the natural monopoly question earlier). State-owned companies can use these benefits to engage in anti-competitive cross-subsidisation or in other ways to limit competition in related markets. Private ownership often can act as a spur to embracing normative competition principles, but it does not automatically lead to it. The reason for this is that the political forces that are present are significant forces and cannot simply be wished away by the existence of a notionally independent regulator, and the application of competition laws. Real political power has to be countervailed with real political power.

Continuing state ownership is also a concern where these companies are actively engaged in international trade, for example, if a state-owned enterprise (SOE) from one country is actively engaged in pursuing privatisation opportunities in its sector in another country. Where this brings the SOE into competition with private sector participants in such processes, the outcome can be problematic.

Since SOEs very often are essential facilities or own them, this poses an additional risk that they will apply political considerations in their buying decisions, such as where a particular provider will buy only home-grown raw materials. Another concern is that the SOEs can control access to these essential facilities—hence those who need to interconnect into such facilities can experience great difficulty in doing so. Regulators have found it hard to ensure competitive interconnection (see Telmex case).

Notes

1 John Nellis and Sunita Kiheri, *Privatisation in Competitive Sectors, the Record to Date*, Working Paper 2860, World Bank, June 2002.
2 *See*, for example, W.L. Meggenson and J.M. Netter, From State to Market: A Survey of Empirical Studies on Privatisation, 39 J. Econ. Lit. 329 (2001).
3 Asian Development Bank, *Special Evaluation Study on the Privatization of Public Sector Enterprises: Lessons for Developing Countries*, Asian Development Bank, December 2001, www.adb.org/sites/default/files/evaluation-document/35461/files/ses-public-sector.pdf.
4 *See Id.*, at 24.

5 David E.M. Sappington and Joseph E. Stiglitz, Privatisation, Information and Incentives, 6 J. of Pol'y Anal. Mgmt. 567 (1987).

6 *See* CSO, *U.K. Public and Industrial/Commercial Companies: Net Surpluses and Rates of Profit*, CSO, 1996. Source.

7 Margaret Thatcher, *The Downing Street Years*, HarperCollins, 1993.

8 *See* Department of Energy, Energy Information Administration, *Annual Outlook for US Electric Power*, Department of Energy, Energy Information Administration, 1985; Department of Energy, Energy Information Administration, *The Changing Structure of the US Electric Power Industry 1970–1991*, Department of Energy, Energy Information Administration, 1993. *See Annual Outlook for US Electric Power*, 1985 and *The Changing Structure of the US Electric Power Industry*, 1970–1991, www.eia.doc.gov/cneaf/electricity/;age/electric_kid/append_a.html.

9 *See*, for example, An Examination of H.R. 3890, A Bill to Reauthorize the Metals Program at the Department of Energy: Hearing Before the Subcomm. on Energy, H. Comm. on Science, 108th Cong. 16–21, statement of Douglas Faulkner, Principal Deputy Assistant Secretary of Energy, ff.

10 *See* Jochen Steinhilber, *Millennium Challenge Account: Goals and Strategies of US Development Policy*, FES Briefing Paper, Friedrich Ebert Stiftung, 2004.

11 *See*, for example, Rauf Gönenc, Maria Maher, and Guiseppe Nicoletti, *The Implementation and the Effects of Regulatory Reform Past Experience and Current Issues*, OECD Economics Department Working Paper No. 251, 2000, ff1.

12 *See* USPS Pro Cycling Team, *United States Postal Service*, 2001, https://about.usps.com/postal-bulletin/2001/html/pb22050/A-Fx.html.

13 *See* Jerry A. Hausman, *Valuing the Effect of Regulation on New Services in Telecommunications*, Brookings, 1997, ff.

14 *Id.*

15 William N. Evans and Ioannis Kessides, Structure, Conduct, and Performance in the Deregulated Airline Industry, 59 S. Econ. J. 450 (1993).

16 Richard A. Posner, National Monopoly and Its Regulation, 21 Stanford L. Rev. 548 (1968).

2 Competition and Regulated Industries
Electricity and Gas

We introduced a discussion about the privatisation of the electricity sector globally in the first chapter and drew out some general trends. We will now look at how competition was introduced, and what the impact of the regulatory design was on competition in the specific case of the UK which was one of the first countries to engage in electricity privatisation. We will then look at specific examples in certain other countries.

The impact on trade of these processes is significant to certain regions of the world, where energy companies are competing to serve global and regional markets. This interface is being particularly keenly felt in the European Union, as the energy market has been opened up to competition from energy firms all over the European Union, coupled with the pressure of competition with state-owned or state-led companies. The terms under which such international competition takes place depend on how those industries have been liberalised not only to international but also to domestic private investment.

We will examine how such opening occurred and what this means for international trade in these services. Much of this analysis will be drawn from markets where there has been significant liberalisation, in the UK in particular, but also in Europe.

Generation

We have already noted that competition in generation in the UK privatisation was limited by the fact that there were only two generators initially. The resultant duopoly did not lead to downward pressure on the cost of generation, as had been initially hoped for. In the electricity area, the price of electricity is very volatile because electricity cannot be stored. There is also a nonlinear relationship between declared capacity and peak demand.[1] This means that slight changes in capacity by the generators have significant impacts on the price. This opens the door to potential tacit collusion, as well

DOI: 10.4324/9781003360476-2

as other potentially anti-competitive practices by the generators because of the high rewards that accompany such practices. In addition, if there is insufficient generation capacity in the market, there is then a significant risk that capacity will fall to levels that lead to blackouts which leads to criticism of the privatisation process (as happened in California, see post).

In common with other services and network industries, liberalisation is very contentious and political realities cannot be ignored. That said, governments have a tendency to allow these political concerns to trump other concerns. An example of political considerations trumping competitive concerns occurred in the UK privatisation of electricity, where political considerations meant that the electricity distributors, the regional electricity companies (RECs) were forced to sign contracts for coal at inflated prices (British coal was additionally protected by a tariff). These increased prices were simply transferred to the consumer. The RECs which purchased electricity from the generators through the electricity pool constantly argued for greater competition at the generator level. They were reacting to two distinct problems—one was the lack of competition at the generator level, and the second was the forced acquisition of raw material at an inflated price. When prices rise, publics often demand price caps. However, price caps as we shall see have a tendency to force firms to exit the market and this leads to less efficiency, more cost and ultimately less supply. The price cap was partially responsible for the blackouts and brownouts in California (see post).

After privatisation, the regulator sought to discipline alleged abuse of market power by the generators. A 1993 referral to the MMC led to the following:

1   A price cap regulation; and
2   Divestiture of some facilities to new entrants in the generation market.

By 1998, their market share had dropped to 39%, which was no longer in the danger zone of having market power. However, the terms of the sale of the divested assets were not a straightforward sale, but rather included an earn-out clause whereby the buyer agreed to pay the seller additional monies proportionate to the power generated by it. The problem from a competition standpoint with the earn-out clause was that it created a built-in disincentive to increase supply in line with market forces, leading to an increase in price and reduction of output. The new entrants had basically been required to buy-in to this market dynamic as the price for entry. This led to a total failure of the entry of new generators and the hoped-for competition at the generator level took much longer to materialise than hoped for.

Competition at the REC Level

The role of the continuing trade protection of the coal industry in the form of high tariffs continued to have consequences. Various subsidies and taxes were imposed by the UK government that were designed to promote otherwise uncompetitive coal. If supply competition could be increased, then this favouring of coal by the government would become increasingly untenable. This was very important for consumers because the RECs, and others historically were merely passing their increased costs because of these public sector restraints on competition to consumers. Increased competition at the REC level would make it more difficult for them to do this, unless there was collusive activity (i.e. an agreement among all RECs to pass on these costs).

In September 1998, a plan was put in place to allow consumers to choose their own supplier. However, switching was not adequately achieved (unlike in gas, when 30% of customers switched in response to a 15% price reduction). The reason that switching was difficult in the case of RECs was partially due to the geographic nature of this phase of the privatisation, where customers were essentially confined to purchasing from particular regional electricity companies.

Government Ownership

In the UK electricity privatisation, the government maintained a golden share which prevented any takeover activity. When these shares expired there was a takeover wave where a number of US entities acquired the UK RECs. The impact of the golden share was to take away some of the intended benefits of the privatisation. Part of the privatisation process, as we have noted elsewhere, is to ensure that competitive forces can operate freely and shape the market. One aspect of these forces punishes managers who make wrong decisions or who are inefficient. The government's golden share prevented the threat of takeover which is a powerful discipline on management. Golden share regulations tend to limit the ability of competitive forces to properly shape markets.

The other aspect of government ownership also applies to the takeover process. In the case of the UK, many of the RECs were taken over by companies from other countries that also had substantial government control. This means that an attempt to instil the competitive forces of the market at the supply level are partially compromised, and illustrates another vital link between trade and competition. While in the above example we see government ownership operating as a restraint on competitive activity, in the case of takeover by other government-owned businesses, there is a case to be made that such a takeover may exacerbate the anti-competitive practices that privatisation was intended to improve.

Vertical Integration

The purpose of the privatisation was to build in structural separation of the different functions of electricity production and supply, but anti-competitive forces are always at work and in this case were rebuilding the original integrated structure of the electricity supply industry. Here, an appropriate application of competition policy was key. If vertical integration led to diminished competition in the electricity pool, then consumers would be damaged. However, if the pool already was anti-competitive and the separated structure led to a mark-up at each different level, then vertical integration could be positive. The question will be in any vertical integration model, what impact would this have in terms of potential market power for the generators in setting price and preventing entry.

When the MMC reviewed the potential for vertical mergers involving the two generators, there was a dissenting report that was concerned about the impact of the potential merger on competition. The specific concern was that the generators would be able to keep pool prices high, while targeting the customers of new entrants with very low-price deals. In this case, the concern is essential that the merger would lead to the potential for anti-competitive cross-subsidisation along the lines seen in other network industries.

What Was the Measurable Impact of Privatisation?

It is clear from the data[2] that the productivity gains arising from privatisation were enormous. When measured by electricity sales per employee, productivity post-privatisation was far greater than the industrial average. The data analysed by Newberry and Pollitt focused on the English privatisation. The same authors looked at privatisation of the Scottish and North Ireland electricity privatisation. The data shows that the structure of the privatisation determines competition and the ultimate gains that would be liberated for consumer welfare.

These separate privatisations are evidence that the actual structure of the privatisation basically determines the competitive gains that might be accrued as a result. While this is intuitively obvious it bears repeating and restressing. Efficiency gains in the Scottish privatisations where there were two generators, and a permanent Government golden share were limited. There was also very little restructuring prior to privatisation. In contrast, in Northern Ireland, generation was placed in three companies, with a separate transmission company, Northern Ireland Electric.

It is pretty clear from the data that it is competition and the pressures that the forces of competition creates that led directly to significant efficiency gains at the generation level. This confirms that privatisation on its own is not a panacea. It will either lead to greater liberalisation or less depending on the regulatory structure. This regulatory structure in terms of consumer welfare optimisation is all-important. In all cases, the price cost margin widened to the detriment of consumers largely because generation was split into a duopoly. Generally, as was the UK experience in telecoms also, duopolies are only concerned about whether their combined actions will lead to new entry or whether new entry can be blocked.

In the UK, one of the factors that limited the early adoption of an appropriate regulatory structure was the industrial policy that sought a larger number of the UK firms than the market would have sustained. One can see this type of industrial policy playing itself out in a number of countries. We discussed in Chapter 3 in some detail the impact of a competitor welfare approach to competition implementation and the negative impact this can have on the overall economy. In the UK, the approach was that there should be a large number of firms as this was somehow in the overall interests of the economy. This was a similar approach that led to the Robinson Patman Act in the US. It comes from the erroneous belief that more competition is always consumer welfare enhancing. That is not always the case. As Harold Demsetz correctly pointed out in 1968, we have no economic theory that says that a fragmented market by itself leads to greater benefits to consumers, and indeed to believe so is based on a misunderstanding of the nature of competition.[3]

Electricity Pools

Because electricity cannot be stored, the great competitive challenge is how to match supply and demand in a time-sensitive fashion. The solution that most countries have adopted is to create an electricity pool into which the generators sell electricity. In Norway, the pool is voluntary, and most trading continues in the form of bilateral contracts. In the English pool there is a central dispatch or point of control, and this has given rise to some anti-competitive potential. However, this is perhaps because in Norway, a substantial amount of electricity is generated from hydropower and this capacity acts to stabilise the market.

In Chile, one significant difference is that the old state-owned system had two companies which were then privatised into five separate generating companies and eight distribution companies, leaving much less scope for anti-competitive practices. Large end-users with a demand above 2 MW can have direct negotiations with generators, in addition to the existence of a spot market. The other significant difference is the negative impact this can have on the overall economy. Chile, like Norway, generates a significant percentage of its electricity from hydro power. There is a formula (as opposed to a cost-based) price cap, which leads to a great incentive to reduce costs. This aspect of the Chilean privatisation is worthy of note. Unlike the UK privatisations, the formula-based price cap does allow competitive forces to apply downward pressure on costs.

In Argentina, there is a wholesale electricity market. Unlike in Chile, CAMMESA which controls the wholesale market has significant governmental input through the Secretary of State for Energy's 20% of the vote on the CAMMESA board. Argentine relies on price cap regulation, which itself is problematic in terms of securing efficient and competitive markets.

In Australia, there was much more involvement of the competition agency, the ACCC. Indeed the framework for the electricity regulations was largely set by the ACCC. Australia managed to avoid an uncompetitive generation market (e.g., the State of Victoria has four large generating stations). The ACCC has done a very effective job of communicating normative competition principles to other agencies of the Australian government and other Australian sectoral regulators. In part, this has been achieved by having the ACCC as a broad regulatory umbrella, with the sectoral regulators operating within it.

As we have noted elsewhere, Australia's competition agency, the ACCC plays an important role in regulatory reform and was able to deliver a more pro-competitive market (by, e.g., creating a national pool like the UK). Australia, as part of its competition and deregulatory process, has a Productivity Commission which has stated that average real price has decreased by 21% since 1991 (equivalent to a 1.25% increase in GDP).

The US Example

In the US, a system of vertically integrated geographic (by state) monopolies becomes deregulated, initially as a result of the Public Utilities Regulatory Policies Act, 1978, which opened the wholesale generation market to independent power producers. The utilities were forced to deal with the IPPs through a system of agreements at avoidable cost. The 1992 Energy Act encouraged wholesalers to purchase from a number of different generation options, including those that were far away. This created a market for the wheeling of that power over the grid system. This increased the possibility of bringing on stream cheaper new capacity, which should have had the effect of depressing costs and lowering price. While much has been written about the failures of the California electricity privatisation, one initially positive step was the concept of "retail wheeling." Under this concept consumers could enter into direct contracts with generators. However, it turned out that price setting could still take place in an uncompetitive fashion in the generation market.

The California electricity privatisation is a good example of what can happen when competition issues are ignored when a privatisation goes ahead, or when unrealistic options are chosen for competition policy. In the California privatisation, competitive forces were introduced into the wholesale market, but regulation of the retail market was maintained.

As a result of the privatisation, the remaining utility monopoly still acted in a number of anti-competitive ways that forestalled competition.

1   The transmission monopoly could be used as a bottleneck to prevent available low-price electricity from being wheeled from out of state.
2   In California, there was little real deregulation and competition at the generation level. The use of low retail caps, which as an attempt to keep prices low, merely shifted competition and led to monopoly situations with the low cap acting instead as a floor.
3   California's deregulation actually led to an increase in state intervention in electricity transactions.
4   The failure to create a competitive generation market meant that no new firms entered the market. This meant that California became a net importer of electricity.

The restructuring of California's electricity market was really an ordered competition which tends not to be an effective way of building real competition into the market. A key problem was the fact that power generators sold electricity into the public exchange which set up an anti-competitive bottleneck which led to expanding prices. The public exchange has even used natural monopoly argument to justify its existence.

The major stumbling block was the precise way that price controls operated.

In California, price controls led to the discouragement of new firms from entering the California market. Since electricity rates had been cut by 10% at the beginning of privatisation, the potential for switching was severely limited. California's law also required new entrants to effectively pay for the debt inherent in the stranded assets by making them buy a "Competition Transition Charge." This operated as a tax on consumers and is not unlike the situation in other industries where new entrants are forced to pay a tax to the incumbent so that it can satisfy its universal service obligations.

In addition to limiting the potential for switching, price caps also lead to limits on an investment, thus disincentivising new entrants in the first place.

The fear of rising prices (and their political impact) can lead to situations where normal consumer behaviour is altered. For example, when prices go up, conservation of energy is encouraged, and energy efficiency is encouraged. This did not occur because of the price caps. Another relevant factor that is not widely considered is the very high environmental burden that California maintains over new facilities for power production.[4]

The other problem in California was that the public sector continued to be involved, post-privatisation in selling the electricity to the public exchange. This involvement of state-owned companies that are not subject to competition discipline mirrors the problems we refer to in other areas of this book (such as postal, telecom). This situation was further complicated in California by the subsidies that were paid to some of the public sector entities which led to inefficiencies in the public entities.

By contrast to California, other US states have had a greater measure of success in making their electricity markets more competitive. Examples include Pennsylvania, Rhode Island and Massachusetts.

Unlike the California privatisation, in Pennsylvania the success of privatisation was borne out by the fact that very high percentages of users had switched to nonincumbent providers (45% of industrial users, 44% of commercial and 18% of residential).[5] In addition, total consumer spending on electricity also declined. Pennsylvania achieved this by not relying so heavily on low price caps, but rather allowed new entry by allowing competitive, market-based pricing.

The Transmission Market

When generation and transmission are structurally separated, the main question that is asked is how to price the transmission service? Here, a major difference between electricity and other network utilities is the laws of physics themselves that dictate that electricity cannot be stored. This makes it much more difficult to match available supply to ever-changing demand. It is this problem that lends support to the notion that electricity is an industry where natural monopoly applies. The alternative view is that contracts can handle these network externalities.

A recurrent problem, however, in particular as was demonstrated in the UK electricity privatisation was the notion that a lack of competition upstream at the generator level could have a profound impact on downstream transmission and distribution markets. If there is a pool into which the generators send power, and that pool is not an open access pool, then these anti-competitive effects can be more pronounced.

The key lesson that seems to come out of the electricity cases is that the entire regulatory design should be focused on reducing the market power of the generators and ensuring adequate competition at the generation level. Without this, anticompetitive effects will sweep throughout the various levels of the electricity market.

The Argentine example demonstrates that even a regulatory framework that looks to be robust cannot necessarily withstand powerful political forces or economic crises. The Chilean example illustrates the importance of applying downward pressure on costs by using a hypothetical benchmark cost for an efficient producer and not allowing the producer to simply submit its costs in a rate of return type regulation.

This system does not allow the forces of competition to result in downward pressure on cost.

In the Review of the English pool conducted by the incoming Labour government in 1997, the focus was firmly on using competition to deliver lower prices. The Review highlighted a number of key factors. The important factors included (i) the market power of incumbent generators, (ii) barriers to entry, (iii) extent of storage hydro, which can reduce volatility, (iv) amount of excess capacity, and (v) extent to which the country has access to cheap gas. Of course, one has to also consider the strength of the institutions that would be involved in the regulation of these issues—the regulator itself as well as the role that competition agencies would apply in shaping the regulatory structure as well as enforcing a pro-competitive regime. This varies greatly from country to country.

In the UK, the Pooling and Settlement Agreement requires that any changes by pool members must be agreed in advance. Since these are often blocked, this led to a very slow-moving market, where incumbents were protected. The main problem continues to be the role that the generators played from their early (1990) duopolistic days. Even after a number of divestitures of coal fired plant, the market did not suddenly become more competitive. The Regulator, OFFER made recommendations in the context of a Review of Electricity Trading Arrangements. The review concluded that the complexities in price formation in the pool meant that generators were able to exercise disproportionate power into the pool, and this led to market manipulation.

In essence the pool did not function as a commodity market would. The recommendation was that the Pool would end, and be replaced by four overlapping markets. These markets would operate over different timescales from real time to forward and future contracts. The question is whether the electricity market can approximate to other commodity markets that involve almost costless transfers and are highly liquid. But time and again, the real problem appears to be the fact that the generators can by acting in anti-competitive ways at the generation level, set forward prices in anti-competitive ways. The best way of securing more competition is to enable a number of different generators to bid into the spot market (as is the case in the Victoria Pool). The need to have an open pool is one of the key policy recommendations to come out of the many reviews of electricity privatisation. The conditions of the electricity markets around the world suggest that what matters is not so much whether there is a privatisation or not, but rather the regulatory structure that surrounds privatisation. Just as in other examples, it is possible to set up a privatisation that has more anti-competitive effects than the previous state-owned sector.

Several years on, there are now six major generator companies operating in the UK. These are EDF Energy, E.ON, RWE, Iberdrola/ScottishPower, Centrica and SSE. However, all told there are about 30 generators. The old transmission and distribution monopoly has also been partially improved. There are now a number of companies operating in this space. National Grid continues to own transmission for England and Wales, but two companies operate transmission for Scotland, and there is a separate transmission company for NI. In addition to onshore transmission companies there is an offshore transmission operator for the offshore wind farms. There are additional interconnectors with France and the Netherlands.

At the distribution level, there are now 14 Distribution Network Operators (DNOs) in GB, and 1 in NI. There are six additional DNOs in GB.

One of the major changes to the energy market in the last few years has been the rising impact of environmental commitments. In 2012, the UK government estimated that 20% of its energy supply would be switched off over the 10-year period from 2012 to 2022. This involves the decommissioning of old nuclear power stations and the switching off of coal fired plants.

A huge investment was required in the UK energy market to ensure energy security (estimated at £100 billion in 2010 over the next 10 years). (much lower levels of investment actually flowed in this time.)

Electricity market reforms did take place in 2013 and there was a Competition and Markets Authority review of the energy sector in 2015.

The Review found a number of anti-competitive market distortions. These include the uniform charging for transmission losses which led to the potential for anti-competitive cross subsidisation. The lack of locational pricing also leads to lack of properly deployed investment.

Regulation in the Gas Sector

Unlike electricity which cannot be stored and fails to safety, gas can be stored and fails to danger. Like electrons, gas molecules are identical to consumers. These similarities and differences drive much of how the gas sector has been regulated. Like the network industries discussed in this chapter, gas is subject to network effects and also to universal service type obligations. However, competition can introduce efficiency gains into this sector like the others.

The gas industry is characterised by very high sunk costs for exploration, drilling and so forth. There are significant investments to be made in exploration, in drilling, and in transportation of the gas in a safe manner from the gas field to the storage facility, and then on to the consumer itself. Unlike telecoms (where competition must be developed from within the overall sector), in the minds of the consumer, gas competes with other energy sources. Those who are incurring the investment costs must constantly bear in mind that if costs increase too much, consumers will switch to alternative sources of power. Gas producers therefore tend to need to develop long-term relationships with pipeline companies. Pipeline companies in turn seek long-term contracts with consumers. The network must move comparatively slowly. Gas has always been treated as a natural monopoly, despite the fact that it does compete with a number of different power sources. Since gas cannot be easily moved between markets, it is relatively easy for gas producers to keep supply low in order to lead to price increases and hence the impact of monopoly is significant. Far from merely assuming that gas is a natural monopoly, one must instead consider the very harmful effects of monopoly which is particularly pernicious in this sector.

Gas liberalisation has focused on dealing with this last point by stimulating the creation of gas spot markets. These spot markets would enable large reserves to be developed with less risk that they will subsequently prove valueless to the gas producers.

There is also a close link with trade in the case of gas, as generally gas pipelines flow through multiple countries. The Energy Charter Treaty was ratified in 1998, which grants national treatment and non-discriminatory provisions for the trading of gas (the "GATT" for gas). This Treaty is meant to allow access. For many countries which are dependent on gas imports, these access provisions are critical. Gas has been very reliant on long-term contracts because gas tends to be concentrated in particular gas fields. In Europe, access issues are now determined by the European Gas Directives of 1998 and 2009.

Relationship Between Gas and Electricity

There is a clear relationship between gas and electricity. The price of one constrains the pricing options of the other. Hence, we can expect some regulatory convergence between the gas and electricity regulators given the fact that the markets interact. In the UK, both regulatory agencies have been combined. This implements the reality that gas and electricity have become increasingly substitutable in both production and consumption. Convergence is also required to ensure that the electricity and gas spot markets work compatibly with each other.

Competition problems arise where gas prices to final consumers are adversely affected by price-discriminating domestic monopolies.

Differences Between Gas and Electricity

While there are strong similarities between gas and electricity, there are also important differences. The principal ones include the fact that gas can be stored, and that gas fails to danger, whereas electricity cannot be stored and fails to safety. The other major difference is that electricity flows at the speed of light, whereas gas moves slowly. This means that gas pipelines may either be owned by the pipeline owner or may be a contract carrier or may be a common carrier. In the last case, the common carrier must give access on a non-discriminatory basis. Gas also does not move in a constant velocity manner, and the fact that this occurs means that gas flow lends itself to market competition.

Key Competition Issues

The key competition issues are: (a) legal unbundling of transmission from supply and marketing, (b) third party access (TPA) to the pipeline. The European regulatory structure considers two forms of TPA—negotiated and regulated TPA as we shall see later in this section.

In the US, the gas industry has been characterised by a number of private companies, as opposed to the state-owned companies that characterise European industry. In the US, pipeline companies had been using their control of a bottleneck to extract rents from both producers and distributors. The Natural Gas Act of 1938 was intended to deal with this problem. In the early 1980s, pipelines instituted special marketing programmes (SMPs) to deal with the fact that their commercial clients were switching to other energy forms. These programmes allowed customers to buy gas directly from producers where they could, and transport this gas via the pipelines. The District of Columbia Circuit Court of Appeals in several 1985 cases found that these programmes were illegal on the basis that they discriminated against those who did not have the power to buy gas directly. The SMP programmes were eliminated on 31, 1985. FERC tried to institute the SMP programme by formally allowing customers to buy gas directly from producers (Order No. 436).

FERC Order 436 (1985) was intended to deal with the continuing effects of monopoly by providing for non-discriminatory open access to transport at regulated rates by enabling customers to buy gas directly from producers. Unlike the SMPs, it applied to all customers. Under the Order, the interstate pipelines could only act to transport gas. The interstate pipelines were prevented from treating transportation requests differently if they came from customers or if they came from the pipelines merchant business. Order 436 represented a voluntary framework, but all gas companies eventually took part in the programme. Under the FERC order, transport rates had to be below the fully allocated cost of transport (and in general were above the variable costs). This order was the subject of some litigation, and ultimately led to FERC Order 636 (1992) which required pipeline companies to unbundle the transportation element as well as storage and give equal access to third party users (and not to discriminate in favour of those who had affiliate relationships with the pipeline company itself). In other words, it made the voluntary programme of Order 436 mandatory. Now all natural gas users equal treatment in terms of moving gas from the well to the customer. This ultimately led to a liquid spot market. It also led to a situation where the pipeline companies became exclusively transportation companies. A number of different pricing patterns emerged which were based on more competitive models. On the ground the whole process led to a fall in gas prices. This competition shortened what had historically been very long-term contracts that led to the uncompetitive market (the so-called take or pay contracts).

The UK Gas Experience

By contrast with the US where the original starting position was a large number of gas suppliers, in the UK, British Gas was privatised with BG owning transmission, distribution, supply and bought gas from other gas fields, as well as owning some of its gas fields. In other words, BG had a substantial monopoly in the production, delivery and sale of gas to its gas customers in the UK. The key problem was that there was no requirement to separate out transmission and distribution which, arguably had the most significant natural monopoly characteristics. There was also no requirement to produce separate accounts for the regulated franchise market and unregulated contract market. This set up the possibility for anti-competitive cross-subsidisation. The more significant problem was that the cost of gas in the regulated sector was determined to be the average cost of gas for all BG purchases, including its very cheap contracts from the North Sea basin. This meant that not only was cross-subsidisation made possible, it was actively encouraged, and in this case almost required by the regulatory system. In an investigation, regulators found that prices were inversely proportional to the ease with which customers could use alternative fuels, and BG selectively undercut potentially competitive gas suppliers. The inventory of BG gas behaviour reads like an inventory of anti-competitive practices, from refusal to supply interruptible gas to some customers, restricting the use of gas to some customers, failure to provide information on costs of common carriage, abuse of dominant position and so forth. It thus demonstrated all the classic behaviour that an incumbent with market power engages in many of the network industries we study. Indeed, the reader will be familiar with this litany of abuses from the example of the Mexican telephony system which we describe in detail. The difficulty the regulator (both sectoral and competition) had with BG was where to draw the line between the regulated core with natural monopoly characteristics, and the unregulated competitive businesses. Without satisfactory accounting separation, it is almost certain that an incumbent will try and divide its costs in such a way that the major costs elements are in the regulated facilities, and the lowest costs are in the competitive business units. This in turn enables the incumbent to engage in anticompetitive cross-subsidisation which is very difficult to prove since the incumbents' costs in the competitive sector (where the predatory pricing claim is being made) is very low. It therefore becomes very difficult to show that the incumbent is pricing below some measure of cost in this sector.

The only satisfactory way of ensuring that this does not occur is to ensure that the different segments of the business are effectively and properly unbundled. There are a number of problems associated with introducing competition even into separated segments.

Competition in Storage and Transmission

The MMC had hoped that competition in storage would have spill over competitive effects. However, in the UK, both significant storage facilities are owned by BG (technically Transco)—the Rough field, and the salt cavity at Hornsea. The other problem was that the demand for storage was coming from Centrica (another BG subsidiary), which handled trading issues. The way the MMC proposed to solve this problem was to have an auction for BG's storage capacity. There was a limit of 20% of storage capacity for any given bidder. The question is whether the transmission segment can be subject to auction as well. One approach is to assume that there is a single pool of gas as the UK authorities have done.

The European Gas Directive

As in the electricity sector, the European Commission has tried to ensure a functioning internal market for the provision of gas. Like the Electricity Directive, the Gas Directive establishes common rules for the transmission, distribution, supply and storage of gas. Its purpose was to improve the security of supply and increase Europe's industrial competitiveness. The 1998 Gas Directive sets out the following core objectives:

1   Establishment of a single EU-wide natural gas market.
2   Improve competitiveness of European energy undertakings.
3   Accounting separation.
4   Separate management of the transportation network from other activities.
5   Increase the power of the regulator particularly regarding transparency and competition.
6   Allow transparent, non-discriminatory public service obligations.

The key element in ensuring a competitive market that the directive deals with is third party access to infrastructure. This requires as a pre-requisite the unbundling of transport/distribution from supply. The directive advocates a regulated access regime. The problem with this ex post facto regime, is that it requires compliance and if there is no compliance, enforcement of the Directive has to be credible. In addition, the key goal was to weaken incumbent domination. Competition in gas also depends on the provision of sufficient available capacity at interconnecting points.

The key elements of the 2009 Gas Directive built on this structure and that of the 2003 Gas Directive by applying common rules for the internal market for gas. The Directive sought to make unbundling much more likely by requiring gas companies not to discriminate against competitors in terms of network access and investment.

Spot market trading was also relied on as a way of ensuring that some competitive forces are operating.

Public Service Obligation

Article 3 of the 1998 Gas Directive provides that Member States can impose public service obligations. These PSOs (in line with the *Altmark*[6] conditions on state aids which require the PSO to be strictly necessary and narroly defined and subject the PSO to certain requirements such as regid accounting separation to ensure the PSO is not used as a basis for anti-competitive cross subsidisation) generally relate to security, quality, price and environmental protection. Article 3 provides that these PSOs must be clearly defined, transparent, non-discriminatory and verifiable. These bear some similarity to, but some importance differences from the *Altmark* conditions. Broadly, they appear to allow more PSO activity than the mere restrictive *Altmark* conditions.

The gas privatisation imposed a regulatory regime which was characterised by a rate regulation based on RPI-$X + K$. X was designed to stimulate allocative efficiency, and *K* was a factor to stimulate investment. Just as in electricity distribution bottlenecks can result in anti-competitive effects at the retail level and prevent downstream price competition.

Access

Articles 14–16 relate to access, and give member states three possibilities: negotiated access based on technical standards; regulated access based on tariffs; or a mixed negotiated and regulated access. All gas generators above a certain production capacity must have access to the system. The Gas Directive requires a 20% absolute market opening.

Most member states have now passed legislation which implements the Gas Directive. Eight states have implemented regulated TPA based on published tariffs, three have mixed systems, and two have chosen negotiated access. As regards PSOs, it is important to note that some member states do not foresee having PSOs at all.

Argentina[7]

There are particular competition issues associated with gas markets in Argentina, because gas basins in the region are located far from where consumers are located and this means that unlike in electricity where production and consumption are connected by a grid, gas pipelines often spanning considerable distances. Gas prices are therefore set by local market pricing. This raised the issue that the slow transportation of gases itself causes a problem in delivering competitive markets when consumers and supply are separated by long distances.

Gas markets are integrating in South America, largely due to the large supply of gas in Bolivia. Bolivia supplies gas to Argentina in the amount of 5% of the Bolivia's Gross National Product (GNP). More recently, Bolivia started sending gas to Brazil as well. The private sector also started to integrate.

The gas sector was vertically separated by a law, enacted in 1992. The 1992 law divided the state-owned state gas company into two transport companies, and nine distributors. Open access to the networks is a vital factor in ensuring a competitive market and lower downstream prices. The regulatory system also ensured that new pipelines could be constructed to bypass existing networks. This also meant that companies could use suppliers outside their geographical areas. In Argentina, the number of companies that did this increased dramatically (from 4 in 1993 to 149 by 1999).

A key point in the gas cycle is the point of injection into the pipeline. Here you have gas producers on the one side, and gas distributors and traders on the other side. This represents a point in the gas cycle where anti-competitive activities can lead to distortions in downstream markets.

In Argentina, there are, in addition, problems at the distribution level, where gas customers are free to choose a supplier, but are captive and locked in to a particular distributor. Distributors may engage in cross-subsidisation between that part of the market where they can raise prices to captive consumers, and lower them for free to choose customers. This type of activity can lead to anti-competitive pricing which distorts the distribution market. Distributors who are able to merely pass on the acquisition costs of gas to their captive consumers will not put downward pressure on those acquisition costs. Argentina is unique in its use of gas in that a very high percentage of Argentina's total energy demand is met through gas—47% (see Bondorevsky and Petrecolla, 2001), compared with much lower percentages in Brazil (3% in 2001, or 7% in Chile (1994). Since most of the consumers who buy gas are residential consumers who are captive to particular distributors, the consumer welfare impact of anti-competitive distribution practices is more significant for Argentina than for other countries. However, it should be noted that natural gas use, particularly in energy production, is increasing rapidly in both Brazil and Chile.

Impact of Cross-Border Trading

Chile has a much more competitive market for purchase of natural gas from Argentina than Argentina has domestically. Hence, when Chile purchases natural gas, it awards the contracts to the lowest bidder which puts downward pressure on costs. This downward pressure leads to differences between gas prices as between Argentina and Chile. Furthermore, export contracts in Argentina prevented resale and this meant that the Argentine market was insulated from the effects of low-cost pricing in the Chilean market. By preventing arbitrage, these clauses allowed anti-competitive practices in the Argentine gas market to persist, rather than being limited by the reality in other neighbouring markets. It is clear that any further integration of the gas market in South America would be limited by these kinds of restrictions. Clearly in order to advance towards more competitive markets, there would need to be an increasing number of pipelines across the region to ensure greater levels of horizontal integration. Vertical integration between elements of the gas and electricity markets is also possible, given that gas is used in Chile as a way of generating electricity which feeds into the overall power grid. Hence increasing competition can have a positive effect on these markets also. The key elements in this integrated market include non-discriminatory treatment and provision for third party access. As these are worked out in the different markets in South America, this will require both the tools of domestic competition enforcement and the tools of trade agreements to ensure national compliance.

Since gas is traded across borders, there are also impacts of this trading that further exacerbate competitive problems. We are beginning to see the impacts of this in the gas markets of Europe, the Central Asian countries and the former CIS countries.

Colombia Natural Gas Market

The deregulation in Colombia's natural gas sector led to vertical separation of businesses, and an independent regulator (although policy supervision was retained by the Ministry of Mining and Energy). Recognising that competition institutions were weak in Chile, there were rigid rules on vertical and horizontal separation.

Colombia illustrates the difficulty associated with weak competition agencies attempting to manage the transition from a highly regulated environment to a competitive one. Even in the Colombian case, where the regulatory framework mandated a high degree of structural separation, competition problems remained and prevented consumer benefits from properly flowing from the deregulation.

Common Themes and General Principles

The cases reviewed earlier demonstrate some common themes. One theme is the difficulty in getting to fully competitive supply or generation markets. Ensuring competitive forces operate in the supply/generation sector is key. As regards transmission and distribution, it is imperative to have a pro-competitive regulatory framework in place. Without this, there will not be open access to distribution networks, and the power of the transmission/distribution entity to use the bottleneck to generate anti-competitive results will significantly damage the market, and thus prevent price benefits accruing to consumers.

More generally, the fact that some market segments appear to have "natural monopoly" characteristics and tend to be regulated in non-competitive ways can also lead to distortions. Many regulators, and some competition agencies take the view that in deciding the division of responsibilities between sectoral and competition regulators, natural monopoly segments should be the exclusive preserve of sectoral regulators. So, interconnection and third-party access issues for example would under this thinking be handled exclusively by the sectoral regulator. However, as we have seen in the examples above, the competition regulator ought to have something to say about whether the regulatory goals of interconnection or third-party access policy are being achieved in a pro-competitive or anti-competitive fashion. Indeed, where there are multiple pathways which can lead to the same regulatory goal, it is the competition agency which can determine whether the least damaging pathway is chosen from a competition standpoint.

The type of regulation that is chosen over price in the "natural monopoly" segment also has serious market consequences. Cost-based regulation differs from other methods of regulation in that it tends to reward efficient providers less than price cap regulation. A price cap yields significant rents to efficient firms because the downward pressure on costs is severe. Cost-based regulation is more appropriate to create some downward pressure on costs, but because it is not as severe, it yields less of a rent for efficiency. In developing countries, there may be a greater motivation to correct existing inefficiencies by adopting a price cap, whereas as sectors move more towards the goal of market regulation, cost-based regulation makes greater sense. On the other hand, a price cap has many potentially anti-competitive effects. By arbitrarily setting a price, far from rewarding efficiency, it may promote behaviour which damages consumers (although this type of behaviour is much more likely in the regulated sector). A price cap over monopoly sections certainly benefits new entrants in the unregulated areas, as it prevents the accumulation of the type of fund which can be used to engage in below cost pricing, particularly if the owner of the monopoly section has legacy government privileges that artificially lower its costs, and thereby make it more difficult to discipline below cost pricing. The type of regulation therefore can present a barrier to new entrants in the unregulated sector or be deemed to be problematic for incumbents (which may have invested based on sector opening based on services liberalisation). Hence the type of regulation can create trade tensions between countries. For example, where there is investment in a regulated monopoly coming from the electricity or gas company of a different country, it may lead to government-to-government complaints if a particular regulation does not allow the incumbent to reasonably recoup its investment.

Accounting Separation and Transparency

Accounting separation and transparency is not merely an optional extra, but a very real part of the regulatory process. We have seen from the examples listed earlier and in others elsewhere in this book, the problems associated with trying to demonstrate below cost pricing, a necessary element in showing anti-competitive cross subsidisation in the unregulated sector by incumbents that have a monopoly in the regulated sector. Without adequate cost accounting, competition regulators may simply not get any information from incumbents about their cost base in unregulated sectors, and thus be unable to construct an accurate picture of costs.

This is also true for any regulation of the monopoly segment, where either a price-cap or a cost-of-service regulation does require some understanding of the cost base of the incumbent.

In the case of electricity, there are two levels at which costs must be calculated, first the transmission cost which most countries compute using a hypothetical model to avoid cost inflation by the transmission company (which will tend to increase its cost so as to reap a higher price for allowing others to connect to it). Distribution companies then have their own costs as they pass electricity to consumers. Distributors add to the standard cost of passing through electricity the added value of distribution (AVD). Models for evaluating AVD tend also to rely on hypothetical models as here, the distributor's incentive is to artificially lower this cost. It does this in order to win concessions based on its low pricing. Once again, accounting transparency is required in order to make a proper assessment when the regulator evaluates the bids of competing distributors.

Cross-Subsidisation

In electricity and gas, just as in other sectors, there is a risk that the party that owns the bottleneck facility or "natural monopoly" segment can use profits accrued in that sector to price lower in other related sectors where there is competition. Unless there is complete vertical separation, this is a risk that must be borne in mind in designing a regulatory framework.

We refer to the section on cost calculations for regulated sectors generally. There are a number of ways of calculating cost in the energy sector just as in other sectors:

1   Marginal cost. Generally average variable cost is used as a proxy for marginal cost as marginal cost is difficult to determine empirically. Average cost does not take into account the common costs for those parts of the network that are shared in the provision of a particular service.
2   Incremental cost. Incremental cost does take into account some of the common costs, and long-run incremental cost amortises some of the cost of the common elements over the long run (recognising that some built out infrastructure has replacement costs associated with it in the long run, but not in the short run).
3   Stand-alone costs. By calculating costs associated with the common elements fully, stand-alone costs attempt to approximate the costs of providing a particular service

It is important to note that not all cross-subsidisation is problematic from the perspective of consumer welfare enhancement. Price discrimination, can have beneficial effects for consumers as it tends to encourage efficiency and puts downward pressure on costs. Price discrimination with its positive implications must be differentiated from anti-competitive cross subsidisation which can only have negative impacts on consumer welfare because, being below cost, it is designed to drive out competitors and raise prices to monopoly levels. This also pre-supposes that the party engaged in the predatory pricing has market power in the other sector. This is invariably the case in the electricity or gas sector where transmission is generally separated from other constituent parts of the business.

The 16 February 2006 European Commission Preliminary Report on its competition condition findings in European gas and electricity markets illustrates the powerful interface between trade and competition in this area. The Commission report is designed to highlight areas where anti-competitive practices are causing the energy markets not to integrate effectively. The areas highlighted are:

1   Wholesale markets in gas and electricity are both highly concentrated. This has occurred because of control over gas imports or inadequacy of generation capacity.
2   Lack of new entrants because of foreclosure of access to infrastructure. Incumbent operators use their ownership of key infrastructure to block access.
3   Markets remain national, with very little integration. There is insufficient competitive pressure on incumbent operators and this has led to a reduction in trade.
4   Prices do not reflect supply and demand.
5   New entrants in both the gas and electricity market slack information about access to networks, transit capacity and storage. This is evidence of a general lack of transparency.

Impact on Trade

Increasingly, as electricity and gas markets are being deregulated and privatised, there is an increase in foreign competition. This can take the form of foreign companies seeking to access the consumers in the markets or of foreign companies acquiring providers of these services. These effects are part of the reason to deregulate in the first place as they lead to greater levels of import competition and therefore lower prices for consumers. Since many of the companies being acquired (or even doing the acquiring are state-owned companies) the treatment of SOEs is also relevant.

We have also seen areas which resemble the regulatory issues confronted by other newly privatised industries such as telecom, media, postal and even financial services. We also note that the gas open access rules in both the US and the EU look very similar to what advocates of net neutrality are demanding in the context of the information industries that are driving the new media economy. All of this represents the drive towards a more competitive marketplace.

Climate Change and International Trade

The efforts of governments to deal with climate change and lower the production of greenhouse gas emissions is bringing trade policy directly into conflict with environmental policy. Many proposals have been made in the trade context to deal with these issues. One example is the European Carbon Border Tax Adjustment (CBAM) proposal. This would impose a tariff on certain products produced in violation of emissions rules. Because this tariff is derived from the way that a product is produced, as opposed on outcomes, it pushes up against a fundamental WTO principle that countries should not discriminate on the basis of how products are produced, as opposed to what those products are. To be sure there are exceptions to this general principle, provided that the rules apply to at least all WTO members in order to pass muster under the TBT agreement. But for TBT rules to apply, the ban or import restriction must relate to product characteristics in some way and this is hard to prove in the case of emissions. If the TBT does not apply, the only possible defence to what would otherwise be a clear violation of GATT rules would be an Article XX defence based on the conservation of exhaustible natural resources. Such a defence would be subject to the chapeau of Article XX[8] which requires that it not be an arbitrary or unjustified discrimination where reasonable alternatives are relevant.

In this context, the EU's CBAM is also a unilateral decision by the EU, as opposed to a global agreement which would be more resistant to WTO challenge.

Under the CBAM, the EU importers will buy carbon certificates corresponding to the carbon price that would have been paid, had the goods been produced under the EU's carbon pricing rules. Any price which the non-EU producer can show they have paid for the carbon used in production can be deducted from this. The CBAM is therefore designed to deal with carbon leakage. In order to ensure the CBAM is non-discriminatory the EU will adjust the system to reflect the EU's emissions trading system. Some of the EU companies receive free allowances under the ETS, and the CBAM will only apply to the proportion of emissions that do not benefit from free allowances. The system will go live in 2026, but between 2023 and 2025, firms will have to declare the quantity of goods and the amount of embedded emissions. Initially the CBAM will apply to cement, iron and steel, aluminium, fertilisers, and electricity. After the transition period the scope of the CBAM may be extended further. There are questions which WTO members have raised about the WTO legality of the CBAM. The CBAM could have a significant impact on developing countries' exports to the EU which could erode their ability to develop their economies.

A better way of dealing with the greenhouse gas emissions issue is an agreement between countries in the form of an FTA or a global environmental agreement which makes specific commitments, that there should be a mechanism whereby a derogation from those agreed commitments can be regarded a market distortion. It would then be up to the aggrieved party to prove that this market distortion had a significant or substantial negative effect on competition in a relevant geographic and product market. The aggrieved party would also have to prove causation and damage (as would be the case for any trade remedy), and if all these elements were actually proved, then the appropriate administrative body could apply a tariffication of the distortion which was correlated with the scale of the distortion and its anti-competitive effect. This more forensic approach (than remedies like CBAM) stands a much greater chance of passing WTO muster, and in any event is also more consistent with the spirit of WTO law, as well as feeding into a discussion that is already happening around the topic of Anti-Competitive Market Distortions in any event. This would avoid a special case being made of emissions control which will act as a discriminatory tariff that would have a significant effect on developing countries. The advantage of this approach is also that it can give an incentive to the distorter to bring itself into compliance, as the defendant can make the case that the Anti-Competitive Market Distortion has been removed, or its anti-competitive effect reduced such that there should be a net reduction (or removal) of the tariff. As long as this process can be done more or less in real time, it could become a significantly powerful reform tool.

Notes

1 This is generally accepted, but for a good treatment, *see* Fabien Roques, David Newberg, and William Nuttall, Investment Incentives and Electricity Market Design: The English Experience, 4(2) Rev. of Network Econ. 93 (2005).
2 David M. Newbery and Michael G. Pollitt, The Restructuring and Privatisation of the CEGB—Was It Worth It? 45 J. Indus. Econ. 269 (1997).
3 Harold Demsetz, Why Regulate Utilities? 11 U. Chi. J. L. Econ. 55 (1968).
4 *See* Adrian Moore and Lynne Kiesling, *Powering Up California*, Policy Study No. 280, Reason Foundation, 2001.
5 *Id.*, at 23. Statement of PECO.
6 Altmark, Case C280-00, Judgement of 24 July, 2003.

7 Diego Bondorevsky and Diego Petrecolla, *The Structure of Natural Gas Markets in Argentina and Antitrust Issues in Regional Energy Integration*, Sustainable Development Department Technical Paper Series No. IFM-131, Inter-American Development Bank, 2001.
8 A Normative Framework For Anti-Competitive Market Distortions; Trade and Competition (Routledge, 2023, anticipated).

3   Competition and Regulated Industries

Telecommunications

Introduction

In telecommunications liberalisation, we are closer to the nexus between trade and competition than for many network industries because of the large number of private telecoms providers that have already been participating in multiple rounds of both privatisation and liberalisation, but also as a new entrant in privatised markets. A survey of telecoms markets around the world suggests that liberalisation has not always led to competitive markets. Because of the compelling case for privatising telecoms (above and beyond the case for some other utilities such as water), we have far more examples and data on what happens after the privatisation process, and whether this leads to competitive markets and benefits for consumers. Partly because of this, the telecoms sector was the first services area to be discussed in the WTO context, and was the first services sector to have a WTO agreement applied to it. There is now a period of time—over two decades since most of the privatisations and therefore a track record that can be learned from. The WTO agreement, the Basic Telecommunications Agreement contains certain commitments that countries make to each other, about the liberalisation of their telecoms sector, but also contains a ground-breaking document which many countries have signed up to, the Reference Paper on Competition Safeguards. The underlying reason behind the Reference Paper was the notion which applies not only to telecoms liberalisation but also to all services sectors that domestic regulation can thwart the benefits agreed under the underlying WTO Agreement, and that the trade agreement must provide for ways of locking in reforms that lead to more competitive markets.

Any analysis of telecoms liberalisation must be viewed against the backdrop of the rapidly decreasing cost of telecommunications, arising from technological developments. The difference between the falling costs of provision of the service, and the price which consumers pay means that there are plenty of opportunities for anti-competitive practices and there is

DOI: 10.4324/9781003360476-3

increasing pressure on companies to look for ways to artificially increase their competitor's costs. Prior to the development of other methods of delivering voice telephony, the fact that there was a single public switched telephone network of copper wire meant that there was a significant opportunity, post-privatisation to engage in anti-competitive practices. As this process was rolling out, we also saw international trade rules in the basic telecoms area being promulgated. But now the very rules of the business game that most telecoms providers used to play by have changed. Voice Over Internet Protocol (VOIP) has meant that the conventional telecom model of charging a higher price based on the length of the time of the call and distance over which the signal is carried no longer make sense. A VOIP call can have minimal cost regardless of duration and geographic reach. Old line telecoms companies must adapt to this new reality.

There is significant data on how the cost and price charged have affected penetration rate (telephones per one hundred people). The data suggests that the industry is highly price-elastic, meaning that excessive price has a significant anti-competitive impact. Another difficult overlay is the fact that while telecoms systems were publicly owned, governments sought to maintain high prices for long distance, and international users, while local prices remained low. Politically, it was important for governments to ensure that their voters (who primarily made local calls) were sufficiently happy. The fact that after privatisation, this means that the investor is given a monopoly over local telephony again sets up the potential for anti-competitive activity on interconnection and subsidisation. This can have a financial impact on the economy of the country as a whole because if long-distance and international prices are effectively subsidised, local prices will tend to remain higher than the market would suggest, damaging the bulk of local users. The ability of businesses to use this type of telephony is really part of the overall integration of the global supply chain. The failure to deliver competitive telephone costs in that supply chain can disrupt it and prevent countries from benefiting from it.

Cost-Price Differential and Bottleneck Features

The telecommunications industry has a number of bottleneck features. These include the fact that new entrants have to interconnect with the public-switched telephone network (PSTN), and that telecoms providers must agree different accounting and settlement rates, based on the cost of calls being connected to another operators' network. Historically, these rates have been unknown and were negotiated through a largely secret process. This adds to the potential for anti-competitive activity.

Since there are bottlenecks at both ends of the call, this can lead to a double mark-up and pricing above monopoly levels. This explains some of the disconnect between cost and price in telephony.

Interconnection

As mentioned, new entrants must interconnect with the existing PSTN, and must negotiate a specific interconnection rate. It is in this area that there have been a number of difficulties. We will go through a number of examples, where there has been very high (non-cost based) interconnection which has meant that new entrants have not been able to succeed in the market.

Cross-Subsidisation

Cross-subsidisation is the phenomenon where one part of a business is used to artificially lower prices in another part of the business. This technique is particularly effective where one part of the business is a state-sanctioned monopoly. Frequently telecommunications providers will use their monopoly in the local market to lower prices in the competitive long distance or international segments. Telecoms providers will engage in this activity, because even as the rates are rebalanced, international and long-distance are more lucrative than the other markets.

Technological Innovation

The regulatory structure can also have an impact on technological innovation. In the US, voice messaging, which was available in the late 1970s, was delayed until its final launch in 1988. Similarly, cellular phones could have been introduced in the early 1970s, but were not actually introduced until 1983. The total cost of delay in the introduction of cellular phones has been estimated to be $100 billion.[1] Total US global telecoms revenue at the time was $180 billion, so it can be seen that this number is significant. The fact that the US had a monopoly at the time was a significant reason for these delays. The delays were also caused by the nature of the divesture remedy in the case of *US v. AT&T*.[2]

It is clear that inefficient regulation and inadequate competition can have a hugely negative impact on consumer welfare, and innovation. Competitive markets can eliminate the need for the market intervention caused by excessive regulation.

There have been studies that have been commissioned to look at the impact of competition on the development of innovative technologies. The Australian Productivity Commission had looked at international benchmarking of the Australian telecommunications industry. The Productivity Commission issued a report in December 1998,[3] which found that in Sweden, the fact that the incumbent, Telia did not have any protection against the entry of competitors was a substantial reason that the country was the first to develop a mobile telephone network and was largely responsible for low prices. In the case of Sweden, interconnection was mandated. Sweden had the lowest long-distance public-switched telephone network prices at the time of the study. Sweden's regulatory arrangements also required local loop unbundling in 1997. In addition, a Mason Communications study[4] released in 1996 benchmarked a number of different telecoms sectors for the British telecoms regulators, OFTEL. The Mason study found that a competitive sector allowed Sweden to emerge as a mobile provider sooner than other countries. Competition between the mobile provider and Telia led to much lower prices across the board. By contrast the lack of competition in the US system can be shown to have delayed the onset of mobile telephony. The application of Moore's Law[5] means that there is a huge impact on cost as a result of the application of new technology.

In the telecommunications industry, there has been significant change in the way that the industry functions as a result of technology. Initially there was significant reliance on the public switched telephone network, the backbone of telephony services. The consumer was connected to the local loop usually through a twisted copper pair. This then interconnected with the local exchange. The local exchange was connected through a series of switches to the rest of the network. In this system, once privatisation takes place, new entrants need to be connected to the incumbent's network. Here the incumbent can act in many ways to limit the success of the new entrant in increasing market share. This situation is exacerbated by the fact that in order to encourage investors to invest in the privatisation in the first place, a carveout is given for certain segments of the market, such as local monopolies while long distance and international markets are opened to new entrants. This retention of certain segments of the monopoly allows incumbents to engage in cross-subsidisation that leads to more market distortions and again impacts the ability of new entrants to be successful. This is not to argue that such methods of privatisation are faulty, per se, but rather that the impact they have on competition needs to be guarded against. As in the energy sector, the creation of a natural monopoly core creates the basis for future anti-competition.

However, technology has brought many changes in the way consumers purchase telephony. Consumers may choose between wireless and wire-line, can generally choose what equipment they want to use to connect to the network, and can even choose the connection. Now there is an increasing possibility of using the internet (through VOIP services) to provide alternative methods of delivering voice signals from one consumer to another. Add to this the fact that much information that was traditionally carried by voice is now being carried by data transmission over broadband cable or fibre-optic connections and the internet, and the telecoms choices available to consumers are even greater. The phenomenon of convergence has transformed the media and telecommunications sector, and has opened up significant alternative bypass options for the traditional wired telephone service.

Originally analogue signals were switched by the PSTN to ensure that calls were carried properly. The advent and use of digital signals has meant that most switches now are digital, and digitised signals lend themselves to be transferred by the developing new technologies. This is because digitised signals can be more easily compressed. The result switching technique is called packet switching where packets of information (bits) are stored and more efficiently use the bandwidth available than circuit switching which books the entire bandwidth for a particular operation. The increased reliance on digital signals has opened the door to voice over internet telephony. Digitised compression means that the world of new technology applications is opening up exponentially fast.

Many of the arguments in favour of natural monopoly in the telecoms sector were built on the notion that economies of scope, the need to provide switches that worked well together, meant that the most efficient solution was a single network provider. It was an "analog world" argument which took no account of the impact of digitisation. However, the rise of digital signals has meant that the reasons behind the idea of a natural monopoly are much weaker than they were. The notion that investors in telecoms privatisations need to be protected from new entrants and from competition carries much less weight in this new world than existed in the past.

In the US, telecoms liberalisation began with the breakup of AT&T through the Modified Final Judgment (MFJ) of 1982[6]. The MFJ was a structural remedy for the market abuses of AT&T. However, competition did not develop as intended and there was a continuing need for regulation. New entrants, which did rush to enter the US market did not do as well as they had intended to do. As we have demonstrated the introduction of new technologies such as cellular service was delayed.

There is data that suggests that even in the local market, which has traditionally been assumed the closest to a natural monopoly, conditions for natural monopoly fail in at least 2/3 of cases (Shin and Ying, 1992).[7]

In the US deregulation, there was some understanding of the fact that a number of companies could perform similar services. Thus the 1996 Telecommunications Act expressly stated that cable television companies would be exempt from rate regulation if the local phone company offered video over cable in competition. Under the 1996 Telecommunications Act, the Regional Bell Operating Companies (RBOCs) had to unbundle as far as possible all network components. Competitors then compete through facilities-based competition, where they offer alternative facilities, through interconnecting to the RBOC's network to resell services. The Act stressed complete unbundling of all network elements and used a methodology (TELRIC pricing-*see post*) for cost calculation that together would lead to the discouragement of facilities-based competition.

As with most liberalisations, the key tension contained within the Telecommunications Act, 1996 was the desire to stimulate competition as well as deal with the Universal Service obligation. This is the age-old network industries problem. One way of dealing with this kind of obligation is to provide a lump-sum tax to minimise the inefficiency costs. However, in the US, the tax was levied through mandatory contributions, and included revenues generated from internet companies. Rather than taxing the line rental, the FCC proposed a mechanism that taxed the new and developing technology to in effect subsidise the old technology. This approach was very destructive to the development of competition. We see this kind of taxation solution in many other areas. For example, as we note later in this book a tax on foreign competitors is a favourite method relied on by certain countries in the postal sector. Here countries require companies that compete with the incumbent postal company to pay into a fund designed to pay for universal service. As we note in detail in subsequent chapters, this kind of regulation has a detrimental effect on trade flows, and distorts the market some 30 years on, we see this pattern repeated in many other sectors.

Interconnection Versus Facilities-Based Competition

There is a contrast between the US system as embodied in the Telecommunications Act, 1996, which created a system of unbundling and cost-based interconnection, and the UK system which essentially consisted of the encouragement of facilities-based competition. However, the facilities-based competition that the UK envisaged flowed from the creation of the duopoly between British Telecom and Mercury. Commentators have noted that the duopoly system did not lead to the development of competition, and its main beneficiary was British Telecom (see Armstrong, Cowan and Vickers 1994).[8] The regulatory system did a couple of things that were attempts to encourage facilities-based competition. The first was to not compel charges to be cost based. OFTEL also did not permit BT to install broadband networks. This encouraged investment by competing cable companies. In effect, OFTEL was recognising that the new market dynamic was one of interplatform competition. What OFTEL was trying to foreshadow was the development of these different platforms. The resultant competition led to significant downward pressure on overall costs, a lowering of the prices of telephony in the UK, and a reduction in cross-subsidies. The UK went from being one of the most expensive places for telephony in 1985, to the second cheapest in Europe by 1997.[9]

Clearly the interconnection into existing facilities does ensure that there is no duplication of services. No further restrictions need to be placed on the incumbent other than competition policy in the bottleneck areas and elsewhere. In the case of facilities-based competition, in view of the cost of building out network elements, in the UK a decision was taken to limit the incumbent's access into different areas (such as broadband). This was done in order to foster overall market competition. Whenever a regulator prevents a market participant from entering into a particular business line, observers should rightly be suspicious. This is not the best procompetitive solution and also requires the regulator to be in the God-like position of determining what sectors the incumbent should not get into. Most of these choices by governmental regulators have proven to be wrong. The choice turns on how expensive and how difficult it actually is to build out these network elements crucial in facilities-based competition. The combination of Moore's Law and new technological developments means that the cost and time taken to do this is exponentially decreasing.

The most problematic issue in interconnection is the determination of the price at the access point. This has proved most problematic because of the market power of the incumbent at the bottleneck. It is here that the regulator must demonstrate both the most effective regulation to ensure competitive outcomes, but also must face down the not inconsiderable political power of the incumbent. The question then becomes which regulator should be charged with handling these kinds of issues, the telecoms regulator or the more general competition regulator. We would argue that both regulators have something to say in this discussion. The competition regulator is in a better position to look at different behaviours and determine their impact on the market, whereas the telecoms regulator is in a better position to look at the specifics of interconnection pricing, and come up with mechanisms to determine what costs should underpin interconnection pricing. The competition regulator is in a better position to discipline anti-competitive practices, from a political standpoint because of the lesser likelihood of regulatory capture (see discussion in other chapters). We will see the impact of this effect in some other markets where foreign new entrants had found interconnection difficulties.

Rebalancing

In most countries, there is a political desire to keep prices for domestic telephone traffic, particularly local traffic low. When the telephone company was a state run monopoly, this was straightforward. However, after liberalisation, many countries preserved the state mandated monopoly in local, and allowed competition into the long distance and international markets. This led to lower revenues for the phone company unless they increased their local prices, something that was politically sensitive. This process is known as rate rebalancing. The danger with rate rebalancing is when it becomes overbalancing. It is possible for a telephone company to increase its local rates to the level, where some revenues can be used to cross subsidise much lower rates in long distance and international, rates that could be designed to drive the new entrants out of the market or render them unprofitable. Indeed, this type of rebalancing has indeed occurred in many countries, such as Mexico by way of example.

Having looked at some of the key economic drivers in the industry, we will now review what international trade rules say about it.

WTO Basic Telecommunications Agreement and Reference Paper

The first sector specific agreement negotiated under the GATS framework was the Agreement on Basic Telecommunications. The agreement (or annex) was an attempt to ensure that barriers in the telecoms market were properly dealt with. The major barriers that new entrants face in accessing these markets had been in the domestic regulatory policy of other countries. These policies had thrown up a number of roadblocks to new entrants, but they did not operate like traditional barriers that violated the WTO's injunctions against discrimination. These barriers were instead pro-incumbent barriers that adversely affected the ability of new entrants to properly access these markets. Incumbents having lost the ability to totally forestall entry, shifted their focus to lobbying for regulatory provisions that protected their business.

When the new entrants sought to eliminate these barriers through trade agreements, this raised an interesting political dynamic. Some of the most outspoken new entrants were also incumbents in their home markets. It was not unusual to see different views expressed, depending on which side of the company was expressing them.

Members of the WTO agreed to binding commitments in the provision of basic telephony services as part of that set of agreements in 1997. Many countries made differing commitments according to which were set out in the agreement itself at the horizontal level, and in the detailed schedules to the Agreement.

At the horizontal level, the Basic Telecoms Agreement is based on the broader GATS agreement, which included disciplines on national treatment and MFN as all WTO agreements do.

Scope of Basic Telecoms Agreements' Commitments

Each member is required to ensure that any telecoms provider from another member must be able to have access to the public basic telecoms system on reasonable and non-discriminating terms. This coverage includes all methods of access, including telephone, telegraph, telex and data transmission, through leasing interconnection equipment, to connect private system with public system, transmission of data over the public system. Some countries also made commitments for value-added service.

The sector specific commitments of the Basic Telecoms Agreement parallel the services schedules of other GATS sectors which we discussed in detail in the chapter on services. First countries make commitments in certain telecoms service subsectors, such as voice or data transmission, or with regard to ISPs.

While there is no definitive list because negotiators recognised that changes were being made in a very dynamic and innovation sector, it was agreed that negotiations would cover:

1   Simple transmission. This would include international and domestic telephony, data transmission, telex, telegraph, facsimile, private leased circuits, satellite services, mobile services and video transport services.
2   Infrastructure.

Note that basic services are different from value-added or enhanced services, such as e-mail, voicemail, on-line information, database retrieval, data processing and electronic data interchange. In some cases, these are already subject to Uruguay Round commitments.[10]

Recapping our specific analysis of how to read a GATS schedule, the commitments that countries make are broken down in the following ways:

a)   National Treatment Commitments. These are the commitments where a country agrees that in its treatment of particular kinds of services, it will not discriminate against the service providers of another country.
b)   Most Favoured Nation commitments. These are the commitments where a country agrees that any treatment it gives to another service provider it must give to providers of all other WTO Members.

Both of these broad provisions apply very specifically to the four modes of service delivery. These four modes of service delivery are:

a)   Mode 1: Consumption Abroad. This mode applies to services which are consumed in another country. It is the most basic of the modes of service.

b)   Mode 2: Cross-border supply of services. This applies to the case where services are produced in one country and sold to consumers in another country, where the service is provided across borders.
c)   Mode 3: Commercial presence. This mode applies to services where the service provider of one country seeks to set up a commercial presence (e.g. subsidiary or branch office arrangement) in the other country.
d)   Mode 4: Temporary movement of persons. This mode applies to persons who the service provider of one country wishes to send to other countries to set up services.

Hence countries, picking certain subsectors can, for example, say that they agree not to impose rules or regulations that would discriminate against foreign providers of that particular service with regard to commercial presence. This would be a bound Mode 3 commitment for national treatment. In the cases listed later, all of the countries made commitments in various sectors and various ways.

Reference Paper

As described earlier, the Reference Paper contains a basic set of minimum standards regarding pro-competitive regulation. The Reference Paper was the first of its kind in the WTO context. In addition to the usual MFN and national treatment provisions, the Reference Paper also provides for certain pieces of pro-competition regulation which while certainly helping foreign new entrants could also be particularly helpful to domestic new entrants as well. The Reference Paper thus recognises the reality of the new trade and competition interface. The core of the Reference Paper includes the following areas which mirror the areas where many disputes have arisen. These focus on core areas into which competition should be introduced. In access, which includes interconnection and access to unbundled and value-added services, the Reference Paper notes that such access must be granted on a non-discriminatory basis. Interconnection must be cost-oriented, as well as having non-discriminatory rules applied to it.

The notion of "cost-oriented" interconnection was itself part of a compromise. Many delegations wanted "cost-based" as the term which represented the interconnection obligations. Cost-based was more reflective of a pro-competitive outcome, whereas "cost-oriented" could include other elements that could nevertheless allow the incumbent company to engage in anti-competitive practices. The closer that the interconnection price is to cost, the less scope there is for the incumbent to use that price to engage in anti-competitive cross-subsidisation in other market segments.

The Reference Paper also contains disciplines on anti-competitive cross-subsidisation. The Reference Paper is intended to ensure that the investment and fair access that was supposed to follow the new WTO norms in the telecoms area was not forestalled by regulatory failure or regulatory protectionism. The Reference Paper was required because national treatment and free trade alone would not guarantee a competitive market in the telecoms sector. The Reference Paper also focused on the role that "major suppliers" play in the market. The notion of "major suppliers" is naturally tied to the competition concept of dominance or market power. These provisions make the Reference Paper much more of a competition policy document than a trade document in the traditional trade sense. By looking at the market effect of the supplier, the Reference Paper moves away from the pure National Treatment and MFN approach of previous trade agreements. Now regulation that violates the Reference Papers provisions governing "major suppliers" can have an equally pernicious effect on both foreign new entrants to market and domestic ones. Clearly if regulation leads to a market impact on domestic new entrants, it will naturally also damage foreign new entrants and thus be a trade barrier, but it is a trade barrier without necessarily being discriminatory.

The Reference Paper also includes specific provisions regarding essential facilities. It draws on both European and US concepts of essential facilities, and it is important to spend some time understanding how the doctrine of essential facilities has evolved over the years. This is particularly important in a world of rapidly changing technologies. It also mirrors the approach of some who advocate that intellectual property is an essential facility.

Evolution of the Essential Facilities Doctrine

We have discussed the essential facilities doctrine in Chapter 3 and also in Chapter 11 on intellectual property[11] as it applies to a number of different contexts. To recap in the telecom's context, the essential facilities doctrine suggests that there are facilities which are controlled by particular entities which cannot be replicated by those firms that are seeking to offer the same or similar services.

However, as we discussed in Chapter 3 of A General Theory, it is necessary to be careful not to apply the essential facilities doctrine too broadly. The doctrine is intended to apply only to those facilities that are truly essential and cannot be replicated.[12] An overbroad application of the essential facilities doctrine will stunt innovation as those who need to make substantial sunk cost investments in infrastructure would not be able to do so under a broad essential facilities doctrine. There is a fine balance to be applied here between the interests of competitive companies and the owner of a network that has invested substantial sums to maintain it.

The doctrine of essential facilities has been differently interpreted between the EU and the US, and that under the US antitrust concepts, the notion of essential facility as analysed under the *Trinko*[13] case has been limited to only those facilities that are truly almost impossible to substitute. The Supreme Court found in the *Trinko* case that Verizon had no duty to share its network with competitors. In the case, Curtis Trinko representing AT&T customers complained that Verizon had a duty to share its essential facilities with its competitors. Trinko had complained that Verizon had violated section 2, Sherman Act by (1) maintenance of a monopoly, (2) by anticompetitive means. The Department of Justice, in its brief in the case, suggested that for (2) to be made out, conduct would have to make no economic sense for the defendant, "but for its tendency to eliminate or lessen competition." The DOJ was anxious to set forth some sort of standard for section 2, Sherman violations that was or rigorously based on consumer welfare standards, understanding that disciplining a monopoly where there is no evidence of anti-competitive harm could lead to a damaging impact on innovation. Under the changes brought about by the 1996 Telecom Act, Verizon, an independent local exchange carrier was required to sell unbundled elements of the network to competitive local exchange carriers at costs (AT&T was such a carrier). This process was subject to FCC jurisdiction under the Telecom Act and the FCC had found that violated its Telecom Act imposed duty. Trinko sought to use that as grounds for a section 2, Sherman Act complaint. Without making express comments about the essential facilities doctrine, the Supreme Court found that Verizon did not fall into ambit of the doctrine because the doctrine was itself a narrow exception to a general rule. Where there are substitutable facilities, even if substitution is difficult, the facility cannot be classified as essential. Refusal to provide access may not have a market impact in terms of consumer welfare, and should not therefore be grounds for a trade or competition problem. These purely domestic concepts must be refined to take into account the fact that parties seeking access are coming from other countries, to be sure, but the fundamental principles remain. Those seeking access from across borders may have higher hurdles to overcome in other areas than their domestic counterparts. These may be because of licensing requirements, or other red tape that domestic companies better understand, or because domestic companies are in better positions to understand the domestic market. This may mean that the essential facilities doctrine could have more of an application in cross-border transactions than it does purely domestically.

It is interesting to observe how the commitments that these countries made in these different sectors are impacted by the competitive conditions in the market place, brought about either by anti-competitive rules and regulations or by anti-competitive practices in these jurisdictions. These areas delineate the scope of the interface between trade and competition issues in the telecoms sector.

Applying the Basic Telecoms Agreement in Dispute Resolution: Telefonos de Mexico

Like the US, the Mexican Federal Competition Commission (CFC), has adopted a proactive role in advocating for the integration of competition policy and regulatory reform. The CFC issues opinions on the impact of proposed regulations on competition conditions that prevail in a regulated market and applies competition policy to specific institutional, legal and economic conditions in specific regulated sectors that characterise each regulated market. Recent examples of the CFC's efforts include involvement in the drafting of the revisions to the telecommunications law and issuing opinions regarding natural gas regulations. It is important that the competition agency has some power to review anti-competitive conduct in order to protect consumers. When an agency does not have the power to enforce its decisions, it is incapable of preventing ongoing abuses. The case study of Telefonos de Mexico SA (Telmex) in Mexico demonstrates this. After its privatisation, Telmex's activities were regulated under the 1990 Telmex Concession, which allowed for competition in certain sectors, in particular the international long-distance sector, while other sectors such as inter-urban and local long-distance were insulated from competition. Telmex was to be regulated in this manner until it could be shown that Telmex had a dominant position in any of these sectors under the Mexican competition law. At this point the regulatory environment changed and an alternative regulatory system was required. In 1998, the CFC did rule that Telmex was dominant in five markets where there was inadequate competition. This ruling was largely ignored by Cofetel (the telecoms regulator), who continued to apply the 1990 Telmex Concession. The problem was worsened, because the CFC had no power to intervene in the decisions of other regulators. The real problem was that cross-subsidisation was allowed by the 1990 Telmex Concession since every time foreign entrants lowered prices in the competitive international long-distance segment, Telmex was able to price at predatorily low levels in this sector, and recoup its losses by supra-competitive pricing in the local markets where there was inadequate price competition. As the head of the CFC has observed, "Regulation has not been able to diminish the dominance of Telmex, and is not being applied concretely. There are a lot of points that are still not applied." The cure to this problem in Mexico would have been that the CFC had greater power to enforce its judgements.

This resulted in a US request for consultation to the WTO regarding Mexico's violation of several GATS articles in the Telmex situation. The complaint, filed 29 August of 2000, stated five main complaints:

1   Mexico enacted and maintained laws, regulations, rules and other measures that deny or limit market access, national treatment, and additional commitments for service suppliers seeking to provide basic and value-added telecommunications services into and within Mexico;
2   Mexico failed to issue and enact regulations, permits, or other measures to ensure implementation of Mexico's market access, national treatment, and additional commitments for service suppliers seeking to provide basic and value-added telecommunications services into and within Mexico;
3   Mexico failed to enforce regulations and other measures to ensure compliance with Mexico's market access, national treatment, and additional commitments for service suppliers seeking to provide basic and value-added telecommunications services into and within Mexico;
4   Mexico failed to regulate, control and prevent its major supplier, Telmex, from engaging in activity that denies or limits Mexico's market access, national treatment, and additional commitments for service suppliers seeking to provide basic and value-added telecommunications services into and within Mexico; and
5   Mexico failed to administer measures of general application governing basic and value-added telecommunications services in a reasonable, objective, and impartial manner, ensure that decisions and procedures used by Mexico's telecommunications regulator are impartial with respect to all market participants, and ensure access to and use of public telecommunications transport networks and services on reasonable and non-discriminatory terms and conditions for the supply of basic and value-added telecommunications services.

Telmex prevented US suppliers from supplying cross-border telecoms services, from obtaining competitive rates for termination in Mexico, and from leasing lines. Termination rates are the rates charged for calls made from abroad whose final destination is Mexico. A USTR press release[14] in commenting on the result of the WTO case, highlights two problems with call termination in Mexico: price, as well as the mechanism for determining the price of call termination. The structure in Mexico allows for only the dominant carrier—who has an incentive to keep prices as high as possible—to negotiate an international termination rate. All other carriers in the country must accept this rate, protecting the rate from competition. This has resulted in termination costs in Mexico being 19 cents a minute, whereas in the US, Canada and Chile, termination costs are 6 cents a minute.

Another serious problem mentioned in both the WTO filing and press release concerns interconnection. By their nature, telecom services have network characteristics. The more significant the network characteristic is, the more consumers will be attracted to the firm with the largest market share. For this reason, interconnection is crucial. On certain occasions, Telmex had outright refused to provide interconnection. Even where it has provided for interconnection, however, the situation is less than ideal. While interconnection rates in the US, Canada and Chile are at half a US cent, Telmex charged 4.6 cents in Mexico.

Furthermore, the complaints against Telmex for anti-competitive behaviour read like a textbook of anti-competitive strategy. These include anti-competitive cross-subsidisation, anti-competitive pricing, discriminatory tariffs to regions where Telmex maintains a monopoly, unregistered tariff and discount plans, requiring competitors to lease unnecessary private lines, discriminatory billing and collection practices, use of information obtained from competitors towards anti-competitive ends, failure to make available technical information necessary for operation, refusal to provide private lines and circuits, denials of private lines to internet service providers, and discriminatory treatment for calls to internet service providers by Telmex. Though the opinion itself has not yet been released in the case, the results from the case have been reported and show that Telmex was guilty of various anti-competitive practices.

Telmex's anti-competitive cross-subsidisation has served to prevent other providers from effectively competing in the long-distance market. The irony is that because of the consequences of these anti-competitive problems, AT&T Latin America was recently sold to its rival Telmex.

There are other areas where similar competition concerns exist regarding the regulations that apply to other regulated industries centred around specific issues related in particular regulated industries.

The Telmex situation is indicative of general problems faced in the telecoms sector, and the need for more successful competition advocacy by the competition agency.

In the case of Telmex, after the Mexican competitor's agency had ruled against Telmex for violations of competition law in five separate markets and the telecoms regulatory had not reacted, the US initiated the first case under the GATS and Basic Telecoms Agreement at the WTO. The case concluded that Mexico had indeed breached the following WTO commitments:

1   its commitments with regard to cost-oriented interconnection rates;
2   its obligation to maintain appropriate measures to prevent its dominant carrier from engaging in anti-competitive cross-subsidisation;
3   its obligations under the GATS by failing to ensure that US carriers operating within Mexico could lease lines from Mexican carriers.[15]

Incumbent Companies and Value-Added Services: South Africa Telecom[16]

It is also useful to review South Africa's telecoms commitments which provided for MFN and national treatment in certain key sectors. These commitments were forestalled by Telkom's anti-competitive practices.

The domestic incumbent telephone company in South Africa, Telkom engaged in certain anti-competitive practices that limit the potential for the development of Value-Added Network Services (VANS). VANS are services that lead to the development and growth of the IT sector as a whole. They include, for example, telecommunications equipment, computing hardware and software, and the consumer electronics industries. Telkom had a statutory monopoly over the telecommunications network facilities in South Africa. These facilities were necessary for the provision of VANS. Telkom was also a competitor in the provision of VANS itself (holding a VANS license). Telkom was challenged for alleged anti-competitive practices that disadvantaged other VANS providers by using its facilities to block the development of other VANS providers. The regulatory process has also been characterised by Telkom's constantly preventing the enforcement of competition decisions on itself through the use of legal remedies that are designed to protect citizens from abuse of government power (something that has particular relevance for the South African environment). This also is reminiscent of what occurred in the Mexico Telmex case, where Telmex relied on the Amparo—a judicial remedy under Mexican law available to those whose constitutional rights are being adversely affected. There is an important point here which reflects the lack of an embedded competition culture.

Just as in the Telmex case, Telkom used universal service commitments to justify its anti-competitive behaviour. In this case, since Telkom could effectively decide whether essential facilities could be leased to VANS providers, it was acting as both regulator and market participant.

It is clear that in this case, the balance of political power lay with the incumbent who was able to use the dual system of regulation at both the competition and telecom regulatory level to manipulate the regulatory process to its own advantage. This illustrated an institutional weakness in the system.

Poland Telecoms[17]

Poland had made certain commitments as part of its WTO obligations. These commitments included interconnection commitments and reference paper commitments. The telecoms system was privatised in 1995, but was unusual in that the incumbent retained a fixed line monopoly in the international sector. Counterintuitively, the local sector was opened to competition, although unsurprisingly the very high market share was retained in local. Market share dropped from 97.97% in 1997 to 93.43% in 2000. This led (see Telmex earlier) to some cross-subsidisation and uncompetitive interconnection policy. The Polish competition law was substantially amended in December 2000, but there was a law in place as early as April 1993. The agency had little if any role in competition advocacy with respect to the manner of privatisation.

In addition, TPSA, the Polish telecoms operator, did avail itself of domestic legal remedies to prevent the enforcement of competition principles (see Telmex, Telkom).

The anti-competitive cross-subsidisation that was engaged in by TPSA was both a competition violation and a violation of the Reference Paper and Basic Telecoms Agreement.

Chile

Despite the emphasis on competition in other sectors in Chile, there were some problems in the Chilean telecom privatisation that has given rise to the failure of many long-distance providers in the country, due to the very high interconnection rates they had to pay to the incumbents.[18]

Romania Telecoms[19]

The Romania telecoms case that illustrates the interface between trade and competition well is the case involving Global One Communications Romania (GOCR), the joint venture between Global One and the Romanian incumbent, Rom Telecom. In the case, Tom Telecom and Global One Communications signed a non-compete agreement for both data transmission and ISP services. They set up GOCR where the parties could not compete with GOCR for 5 years. Under a competition analysis the non-compete agreements had an anti-competitive impact only in the data transmission market (because as of 1999, there were only two competitors, GOCR and Logic Telecom), and GOCR had 70% market share or so. However, GOCR only had 7.04% of the ISP market. Under Romania's Basic Telecoms Agreement commitments and Reference Paper obligations,

Romania had agreed to market access and national treatment obligations in both these markets. A purely trade approach would have found equivalent problems with both markets as Romania's commitments in the WTO were being vitiated by the GOCR non-compete agreements. However, a competition/consumer welfare approach would differentiate between markets where GOCR exercised market power and those where it did not, and find harm only in the former case.

It seems clear from these examples that the benefits of competition only truly flow where new entrants are able to flourish and thereby lead to downward pressure on costs. However, this would have an impact on the original privatisation as this would mean that investors would receive less value. A clear problem is how to deal with the power of the incumbent. In Chile, there was a positive example of the incumbent being broken up in anticipation of the privatisation. This greatly speeded up the introduction of competition into the system. Competition also benefits from lowering barriers to entry. In the telecoms area, one way of achieving this is through number portability. Conversely, rules that make it difficult to change numbers will act as barriers and increase (and thus disincentivise) switching costs.

Type of Cost-Oriented Regulation Applied to Telecom Firms

The two major types of regulation are rate of return regulation and price regulation. As we have noted elsewhere, there are competitive problems with both types of regulation. Rate-of-return regulation does not lead to the kind of downward pressure on costs that can result from allowing the forces of competition to prevail. The problem with price regulation is that although it is based on projected efficient costs, it is still a hypothetical number, and one that a government regulator is not necessarily in the best position to calculate. A functioning, competitive market remains the best form of regulation, provided sufficient safeguards are in place to ensure the market is competitive.

Evaluation of Costs

As is the case in many of the network industries we are looking at, the question of how costs should be apportioned is the key question, and here the devil is very much in the details. Costs are also rapidly decreasing because of Moore's Law and innovation, so whatever costs model is used must be flexible enough to deal with this rapidly reducing cost. The model that has been used most consistently is based on trying to get an accurate proxy for marginal cost. The Long Run Incremental Cost is a base that proxies for average variable cost, itself a proxy for marginal cost. The controversy arises in precisely how the assets of the telephone company are valued. The most used mechanism is the Total Element Long Run Incremental Cost, where costs are based on the elements of the system which are needed to provide the service, and include the total attributable costs of that element, calculated as the incremental cost incurred to provide an extra unit of the service over the long run, in which all costs are forward-looking. The assets are valued at the modern equivalent asset value (MEA). This allows one to lower the value of historically expensive assets which have been overtaken by technology. The problem from the asset owner's standpoint is that this tends to strand the assets. TELRIC pricing is not without its critics. It does tend to make the assumption that networks can be reconstructed using the best technology, which is not always the case.[20] However, the EU in its 8 January 1998 communication[21] on a liberalised telecom market advocated for interconnection pricing based on forward-looking long-run incremental costs. The EU felt this was the quickest way of getting to a competitive market.

The wider question from a distortion reduction standpoint with respect to costs is what impact does this have on new entrants trying to access the system and provide telecoms services. Here there are two considerations. The first is whether the interconnection fee is an appropriately pro-competitive one. Here costs ought to be depressed to ensure that the interconnection price is not allowed to be so high that it prevents interconnection. Incumbents tend to oppose TELRIC pricing because it leads to lower costs than other methods which do not cost elements looking at forward-looking costing, based on MEA values. Incumbents tend to want to also include some element that reflects the costs of the existing infrastructure and incremental pricing does not allow that.

However, costs calculations must also bear in mind that a frequent concern of new entrants is the potential for cross-subsidisation. For that cross-subsidisation to be anti-competitive there must be some below cost pricing. Below cost pricing is difficult to demonstrate. The precise measure of cost is clearly critical in determining if a case of anti-competitive cross subsidisation is present. Including other cost elements leads to a greater probability of funding below-cost pricing.

Anti-Competitive Cross-Subsidisation

Anti-competitive cross-subsidisation occurs when an incumbent uses its power (monopoly or market) in one segment to price at less than some measure of cost in a competitive segment to knock out competitors in that segment.

The traditional way that cross-subsidisation has been analysed has been to look at whether the price that is being charged in the new area can be said to be predatory. The US courts, in evaluating this kind of behaviour across multiple industries, have applied the line of cases culminating in *Brooke Group* to evaluate whether there is predatory pricing or not. We discussed this issue in detail in Chapter 3. The Brooke Group test has a number of elements. To recap, in order to demonstrate that a particular price has negative impact on consumer welfare, it needs to be below some measure of cost, the person charging it must have market power, or dangerous probability of acquiring it, and must be able to recoup the lost profit it incurs by charging the below cost price in the future.

In determining whether there has been an anti-competitive cross-subsidisation, one has to look first at whether there was market power in the related segment which supports the alleged cross-subsidisation. In the case of a telecom's liberalisation, where there is phased liberalisation process and some part of the telecoms market is preserved as a state-granted monopoly, this is a straightforward exercise. Generally, the owner of the network will use that monopoly (typically, though not always in local telephony) to support the below cost pricing in other related sectors. The question is then whether the pricing in the related sector (long distance or international) is below cost, and what measure of cost should be used.

Classical economics tells us that marginal cost is the cost below which a company can only be charging in order to knock out competitors and then raise prices as a monopolist. However, marginal cost is extremely difficult to measure, and economists tend to use a variety of proxies for marginal cost. The most common is average variable cost, which is also not easy to measure. In the case of network industries, long run average incremental cost is a better measure of cost as it uses as cost the cost of doing the next delivery, and does not take into account the very high built-in infrastructure cost which usually is required in most network utilities, such as telecom. However, using incremental cost models does understate the actual cost of the service (by eliminating certain already built out cost elements). Some commentators also include a stand-alone cost criterion, where the cost is solely the cost of producing the service for a particular consumer or consumer group.[22] Problems will incur in ensuring pro-competitive regulation where there is some form of cross-subsidisation and the cost is above some measures of cost (such as the ones listed earlier) but below the costs of other prices. These situations will entail a much deeper understanding and global agreement on what is the most appropriate measure of costs for the telecoms industry as a whole.

Beato and Laffont (2002)[23] suggest that some price discrimination increases net social welfare, but not all price discrimination schemes lead to social welfare gains. They also identify those areas where price discrimination schemes or cross-subsidies are not appropriate from an efficiency standpoint. They consider the following key areas:

1   Clearly prices below marginal cost are harmful from an efficiency perspective.
2   Cross-subsidy driven schemes only increase welfare if they increase the overall level of consumption.
3   A necessary condition to maximise welfare is that the deviation of prices from marginal cost in each market should be inversely proportional to the price elasticity of demand in each market.

For these purposes, TELRIC pricing actually favours the incumbent because it eliminates cost elements due to the built-out infrastructure (because of its forward-looking nature). The new entrant would prefer some measure of cost that adds elements based on the fact that there is already infrastructure which the incumbent has built out that gives it a benefit. New entrants have been successful in arguing that if the telecoms company has some vestiges of government ownership, then the test of what constitutes anti-competitive cross-subsidisation should be refined to ensure (a) that there is no requirement to recoup lost profit (as the government is a revenue not a profit maximiser) and (b) that some elements of costs should be added based on government privileges. The idea of this is to raise the costs of the government in providing the service to the level of a private competitor, and then assess whether there is below cost pricing based on this new model.

The broader question is what impact does the cross-subsidy or price discrimination have on the overall market. The test of this is traditionally based on whether the price is below cost, as noted earlier, and the application of the Brooke Group test.

There is an additional issue which needs to be dealt with when one is looking at recently privatised companies, and that is the role that is played by state-ownership or the legacy of state-ownership. In order to fully explore this area, we draw on the case studies presented earlier.

The Impact of State-Ownership on Cost-Oriented Pricing

State-ownership or the legacy of state-ownership has a number of major impacts on the market economy for the provision of telecommunications services. Where the state is acting as a private party in the economy, it will not act exactly as purely private sector participants would. We have noted many times in this text that the state is not a profit-maximiser. This means that it can sustain practices that are profit-losing for much longer periods than a private company can.

We see that the key areas that come from this treatment are as follows:

Recoupment of Lost Profit

Under the Brooke Group test, as discussed in Chapter 3 in order for a firm to be pricing below cost in a manner that implicated the antitrust laws, it would have to be able to recoup lost profit later. In the case of state-owned companies that are not profit maximising, it should not be necessary to demonstrate this element.

Role of Market Power

Under the Brooke Group test, the alleged predator must have market power in order to be found to have engaged in predatory conduct. The economic justification for this is that if the alleged predator does not have market power, then it will not be able to sustain that practice, as any attempt to monopolise later will be met by new entrants or other entrants simply acting to keep prices down. In that case the alleged predator will merely lose money and no harm will result for consumers. Traditionally, we have used market share as a proxy for market power. However, this proxy tends to break down in high-tech or dynamic industries where the market itself is rapidly changing. In industries such as telecom, new technologies may render old technologies obsolete. This may mean that high levels of market share in a particular product market might misstate actual levels of market power, as new technology might rapidly move to replace the particular products in what was once a relevant product market. The dynamic nature of the telecom's world means that ordinary antitrust principles of product market definition must also therefore take into account the fact that low levels of market share in a particular product might also understate the actual market power that could be exercised if the government entity was able to use legacy privileges to rapidly expand its presence in a particular market.

Rate of Change of Market Power

A snapshot of market share is unlikely to give a good indication of market power if that market share is rapidly increasing. Where market power is rapidly increasing, then market share alone is at best part of an overall evaluation of whether there is in fact a possibility of market power. These factors are rendered more significant when the entity whose market power is being evaluated is government owned or has some significant legacy of state-ownership.

These factors tend to increase the applicable cost that the incumbent generally has for the provision of services. Where the incumbent prices at levels below cost in related sectors, this price may be deemed predatory and may lead to a reduction in consumer welfare and misallocation of resources.

Impact of the Reserved Sector on Pricing: Nature of the Reservation

One key question is what is the nature of the reserved sector. The case studies set out earlier demonstrate two different ways of attacking the problem of the reserved sector. In most telecoms' privatisations, the local monopoly is preserved through the privatisation while long distance and international are exposed to competition. The reasoning behind this is that historically in many developing/transition markets, the local rates were kept artificially low by the incumbents and much higher rates were charged for long distance and international. As these sectors were exposed to competition, rebalancing took place, and local rates were brought up just as long distance and international were lowered. This presented specific issues with anticompetitive cross-subsidisation that are dealt with elsewhere in this text. However, in the Polish case, local was opened to competition first. This was unusual because it would be much more difficult to introduce competition into the local market than the long-distance or international markets where there were many more competitors. Indeed, in the Polish case, the result of opening only the local market to competition meant that the market share of the Polish telecoms company went down from 100% to 93% 5 years after privatisation.

If the fundamental and underlying goal in a privatisation is, as we believe it to be, the introduction of competitive forces, then precisely which sectors are reserved and for how long is a very important element of how that competition becomes introduced. The problem illustrated by the telecoms liberalisation in Poland was that a wrong choice of reserved sector may limit the introduction of competition into the market. Such a limitation may have adverse consumer welfare consequences.

Where this occurs, it becomes unlikely that the country would be able to satisfy its commitments under the WTO Basic Telecommunications Agreement, and the related Reference Paper. Thus, the fact that the reservation is either the wrong sub-sector or overly broad has an anti-competitive effect that means that the country's WTO commitments may be vitiated by this lack of competition. The Romanian case nicely brings out the fact that the same "anti-competitive" practice could have very different effects in the market depending on what market power the incumbent actually has. In the case of the agreement between Romtelecom and Global One, because Romtelecom had very different market shares in the data transmission and ISP markets the effect of the agreement was very different. While competitors may have complained in either sector about the agreement, and the fact that it helped GOCR, and perhaps brought WTO cases under the ISP or data transmission commitment violations under the WTO, competition analysis would say that only in the area where GOCR had market power was there a problem. In other sectors where there was no market power, there was no issue from a competitive standpoint. A purely trade focus would lead to complaints brought in either sector, whereas a competition focus would differentiate between them. Competition therefore presents a more refined and rigorous standard for evaluating whether a particular practice actually has a detrimental or beneficial impact on consumers.

The Impact of the Universal Service Commitment on Competition

The universal service commitment or obligation (USO) is one of the most challenging areas in ensuring a reduction in anti-competitive market distortions. In the telecoms area, the universal service commitment generally applies to any provider of fixed line services. Historically this has been the obligation of the incumbent provider from its earliest days as a state-owned company or even a government ministry. The USO, at that time, was built into the overall business operations of the agency or company that provided telecommunications services under the aegis of government ownership. There was no need to provide a specific fund for these services, because the government had access to taxpayer money to pay for this service, and could use taxpayer money to these ends. Tax funds were so generic that it was impossible for individual taxpayers to complain about whether the funding choices that the government made were an appropriate use of those resources or not. There was therefore little discipline on these choices.

When these state-owned companies were privatised under the wave of privatisations in the 1990s that we have discussed, difficult decisions had to be made about how to fund the universal service obligation. Governments made a range of choices, including setting up special universal service funds. The source of funding for these funds also became controversial. In some countries, the universal service fund was funded by contributions to the incumbent company by competitors of the company, particularly those new entrants that are seeking to access the new market opportunities presented by the privatisation in the first place. In other countries, universal funds were funded by taxpayers, or by a user's fee.

The approach that most countries have applied to the universal service obligation misses the fundamental question that regulators should be asking—what aspect of the service requires universal service, and if so, how much should it cost, and what are its benefits? Many regulators simply assume that the universal service commitment stems from basic human rights for certain types of goods/services. For example, in the case of telecoms, it may be assumed that every citizen has the "right" to access to basic telephony services. While this may be a preferred situation, it is far from clear, without some internal debate, whether this constitutes the kind of basic right that gives rise to a universal service obligation. This situation is to be contrasted with electricity/energy or, in an even more extreme case, water, where the citizen will literally not survive without the service. There needs to be some consideration of the needs basis that underpins the universal service obligation in the case of telecoms, before a USO can be assumed.

Even if the USO is assumed, we must then ask the question, what should it cover? Does USO, in the telephony context, mean rights to a telephone and wireline service? Or does it mean access to telephony services? Does it mean access to telephony services, be they wireline or wireless? Or could it even mean access to broadband or other information delivery services (which is a very different thing from wireline or wireless services)? These are important questions that many regulators do not ask as they lay down USO rules or create universal service funds. The other question that regulators need to ask is what should be the cost of these USOs? Here there are some difficulties because the cost of servicing different customers changes with each customer, and is non-uniform. Hence postulating a USO that is based on the same overall cost of providing the service cannot be accurate. In the specific case of telecom, regulators should instead ask the question what specific services do the public demand should be provided so that universal access to a particular telecom's product can be provided. For example, the public may say that every citizen must have access to basic telephony. In the days before smart phones, this could be accomplished by ensuring that pay-phones were located in positions where people can (reasonably) have access. This might be within a 20- or 30-minute walk, for example. But how is this affected when everyone, even the poorest have access to smart phones and neither want nor need wire-line service? This kind of universal access is very different from immediately creating a fund to pay for the provision of a land-line telephone in every house. Indeed, the Chilean telecommunications privatisation did include specific provisions on universal service, whereby universal service could be in effect auctioned off to lower the overall cost of provision of these services. USO auctions have been suggested as ways to minimise the burden of providing the USO. The USO has to adapt to what is actually needed as technology changes or it will simply become an anti-competitive benefit to the incumbent operator. We discuss this in more detail in the Chapter on Postal.

As we noted in the general introduction on regulation and the USO, regulations supporting a USO must be the least distortive of the market to achieve the public policy goals of the regulator. This is achieved in the telecoms sector by ensuring that there is continuous downward pressure on costs of the Universal Service function, so any fund created under universal service regulation is strictly limited to achieving universal goals and cannot be abused.

The Chilean example also illustrates the difference between an approach based on the fact the goal is universal access as opposed to the goal being universal provisioning of service. By using the language of universal access, the Chilean government was able to craft ways of satisfying the access requirement that would have been wholly impossible under a universal service obligation construct. In the very dynamic market environment that applies to the telecommunications sector, the universal service obligation is a static device that does not allow governments to take into account changing market conditions or new technologies that might make the service to which the USO attaches either obsolete or irrelevant. Changing technologies and the way that information is disseminated may also make the product to which the USO applies not as important as it appeared used to. A classic example of this in the telecoms sector is the role of wireless and wireline. As long as wireline was the only way to provide basic services, the USO was applied to it, even as wireless came in. Now, consumers who need access to basic services can get those services provided by wireless or broadband technologies (and nowadays by a whole other line of technologies), thus reducing the purpose of the USO. It can be seen that a pro-active and procompetitive approach to the USO will be very important.

Where USOs are required without much consideration of the costs of provisioning, they can be abused to benefit the incumbent company. Indeed, the Mexican telecoms privatisation and its aftermath proved to be a good example of what can go wrong. In the case of Mexico, the USO was used as an excuse for low-cost pricing in the international and long-distance markets, where there was competition. By using Universal Service Fund monies to artificially lower costs for the provision of certain kinds of services, incumbent providers can more easily engage in anti-competitive practices that are largely undetectable from an accounting standpoint.

Regulatory Design

As we have noted elsewhere, the regulatory design that applies to a particular sector stems from a combination of the application of specific sectoral rules, and competition policy as implemented by the competition agency. There is a different balance of regulatory power and implementation of competition law in almost every country, and so there is a wealth of examples of what has worked and what has not worked.

There are a number of different options that have been applied in the telecom's cases. These include:

1 Sector-specific regulatory agencies with sole jurisdiction over telecoms matters. This includes agencies such as the Peruvian telecoms regulator. The benefit of this situation is that it encourages sector specific depth and the building of substantive expertise that might not exist in a more generic multi-agency sector. But regulatory capture is more likely.

2 A multi-agency regulatory agency that covers telecoms as only one of the regulated sectors that it covers. This agency benefits from the fact that cross-cutting issues that affect network industries can be analysed and common lessons and regulatory principles can be drawn.

3 Mixed jurisdictional approach from the application of competition policy as well as action by the sectoral regulator. The benefit of this approach is as well as further limiting regulatory capture, it also ensures that the costs and benefits to consumer welfare of particular kinds of regulation can be properly evaluated. Thus, the competition agency can inform the regulator of these consumer effects and the regulatory, while not bound by the competition agency's findings, is nonetheless presented with these findings which should inform its own regulatory judgment.

The Reference Paper approach is now being adopted as part of the Services Domestic Regulation agreement. Initially when the Basic Telecoms agreement was agreed, it was anticipated that there would be a series of similar services agreement with similar Reference Papers incorporating competition safeguards into a number of sectors. This never occurred because of a lack of consensus in the WTO (and perhaps a lack of ambition also). It is encouraging that the Reference Paper approach has resurfaced as a mechanism for introducing competition issues into services liberalisation.

Summary

There is a very clear interface between competition and trade in the telecoms sector. The cases illustrate the interface as well as the danger of applying a purely trade (i.e. national treatment) approach to the problems faced by new entrants into markets. Here one has to have an understanding of how the markets work in order to establish whether there is a problem that will be faced by new entrants and others seeking to have both market access and contestability.

Starting with Article IX of GATS, and the Basic Telecoms Agreement as well as the Reference Paper, we have seen attempts made by aggrieved WTO Members to use WTO disciplines to prevent behaviour by incumbents to thwart the ability of new entrants to enter and be contestable in telecoms markets. Some attempts have also been made to rely on domestic competition law, but neither method has led to market contestability in a timely fashion certainly in a timely enough fashion for it to make a difference to the success of new entrants. The only success stories are for companies that have essentially acquired the incumbent and its privileged status. In the meantime consumers have been harmed. New technologies such as VOIP, and the use of broadband to deliver rapid internet based services to the home has challenged the traditional model that the incumbents have relied on, but this will largely depend on whether they are allowed to freely compete or whether they will be heavily regulated.

A combination of trade measures taken at an international level as well as competition measures taken domestically could be an effective way of delivering the benefits of trade liberalisation and competition markets provided, they can work together in a timely and coherent fashion. It may be that giving the WTO dispute settlement body the ability to refer competition issues back to the competition agency for immediate resolution would greatly help new competition agencies, in particular, deal with the difficulties associated with trying to enforce decisions on powerful incumbent companies. This would also help bring out the competition arguments (in particular the consumer welfare arguments) in the local market which would be helpful in dealing with political roadblocks.

Notes

1 For a good analysis of the impact of regulatory inefficiencies on technological innovation, *see* David M. Newbury, *Privatisation, Restructuring and Regulation of Network Utilities*, MIT Press, 2001. Newbury suggests the $100 billion figure. ff.

2 United States v. American Tel. and Tel. Co., 522 F. Supp. 131 (D.D.C. 1982, *aff'd* 460 US 1001 (1983). ff.

3 Australian Productivity Commission, *International Benchmarking of Telecommunications Prices and Price Changes*, Productivity Commission Working

Paper No. 1611, Australian Productivity Commission, 1999, www.pc.gov.au/research/supporting/telecommuniction-services/telecoms.pdf.

4 Mason Communications, *Benchmarking Studies for OFTEL*, Mason Communications, 1996.

5 Moore's Law states that new technology introduced halves its cost every 18–24 months, *see* Gordon E. Moore, Cramming More Components into Integrated Circuits, 38(8) Electr. (1965).

6 United States v. American Tel. and Tel. Co., 552 F. Supp. 131 (D.D.C. 1982), *aff'd mem. sub nom.* Maryland v. United States, 460 U.S. 1001 (1983).

7 Richard T. Shin and John S. Ying, Unnatural Monopolies in Local Telephone, 23 RAND J. Econ. 171 (1992).

8 Mark Armstrong, Simon Cowan, and John Vickers, *Regulatory Reforms: Economic Analysis and British Experience*, MIT Press, 1996.

9 D. Cleevely, *The UK Market: First Economic Lessons From Liberalisation*, Telecom Convention, 1997, www.analysis.ow.uk/news/1998.

10 *See* World Trade Organization, *WTO Analytical Index: GATS—Annex on Telecommunications*, World Trade Organization, 2021, www.wto.org/english/res_e/publications_e/ai17_e/gats_anntelecommunications_jur.pdf.

11 A General Theory of Trade and Competition; Trade Liberalisation and Competitive Markets (CMP 2007), Shanker Singham.

12 *See* detailed discussion in Chapter 3.

13 Law Offices of Curtis V. Trinko v. Verizon, 560 US 398 (2004).

14 *See* US Wins Telecommunications Case Against Mexico in WTO, Press Release, Office of the U.S. Trade Representative, 12 March 2004, https://ustr.gov/archive/Document_Library/Press_Releases/2004/March/US_Wins_Telecommunications_Case_against_Mexico_in_WTO.html.

15 *See* World Trade Organization, *Report of the Panel* in *Mexico—Measures Affecting Telecommunications Services*, WT/DS 204/R, World Trade Organization, 2004, ff.

16 Singham briefed this case for the OECD Joint Group on Trade and Competition, which reported its findings to the Global Competition Forum in 2004.

17 Shanker Singham briefed this case for the OECD Joint Group on Trade and Competition, which reported its findings to the Global Competition Forum (GCF) in 2004.

18 *See* Pablo Serra, Chile's Antitrust Legislation: Effects on Essential Facilities, in *Competition Policy in Regulated Industries: Approaches for Emerging Economies* (Paulina Beato and Jean-Jacques Laffont, eds.), Inter-American Development Bank, 2002, ff.

19 Shanker Singham briefed this case for the OECD Joint Group on Trade and Competition, which reported its findings to the Global Competition Forum (GCF) in 2004.

20 Robert G. Harris and C. Jeffry Kraft, Meddling Through: Regulating Local Telephone Competition in the United States, 11(4) J. Econ. Persp. 93 (1997).

21 *See* Commission Recommendation 98/195/EC, 1998 O.J. L73/42. ff.

22 Paulina Beato, Cross-Subsidy Prices in Public Utilities, in *Competition Policy in Regulated Industries: Approaches for Emerging Economies* (Paulina Beato and Jean-Jacques Laffont, eds.), Inter-American Development Bank, 2002, 17, at 203–4. ff.

23 *Generally, Id.*

4 Postal Services

There is an increasing momentum towards privatisation and liberalisation in the postal sector. This has an impact on trade in services, especially in related sectors such as express delivery services. This chapter will focus on the impact of privatisation and deregulation on trade and competitive markets in postal and related markets.

The postal industry, while it has many network industry characteristics, does not have the very high sunk costs associated with other key industries such as telecoms, electricity and gas discussed earlier. There are therefore differences in how it behaves from other network industries that help us develop general themes.

Because the postal sector's costs are primarily labour,[1] the natural monopoly arguments deployed in the case of other network industries which we also analyse are less relevant to it. We look at this in particular because of the high level of attention being paid to the postal sector and its reform in many countries. Given the temper of the public debate which is much like the public debate in many countries surrounding privatisation programmes in general, it is important to stress and re-stress the notion that competition can lead to economic benefits for consumers due to the increased efficiencies arising from a privatisation that allows the forces of competition to work through the system, and lead to the empowerment of consumers.

We will look first at the benefits of privatisation and then analyse more deeply the precise impact of the regulatory scheme chosen.

Arguments in Favour of Postal Privatisation

Perhaps the most important argument in favour of postal privatisation is often lost when the issue is discussed. While the argument that the postal company will become more efficient, with resulting benefits for investors is often raised, the impact on consumers of privatisation is often ignored. This is a pity as the benefits to consumers are the most valuable benefits for

DOI: 10.4324/9781003360476-4

society as a whole provided that the privatisation is accompanied by competition as well as liberalisation.

The benefits of privatisation are that public sector monopolistic entities tend not to be as efficient as private entities. It is to be hoped that privatisation will lead to more efficiencies, because managers will be able to keep costs down and quality up. Managers will be able to maximise worker output and minimise waste. These are things that are not easily done in a public sector context. But these greater efficiencies do not just arise because of the fact of privatisation. They arise because of the restraints that competition imposes on managers to perform and also get the most out of their workforce. Postal prices have generally risen in countries where the postal service is a government owned monopoly. This is in contrast to other sectors where prices in communications and transportation have fallen. There is evidence in the US that this number translates into a significant cost imposed on consumers—as much as $4 billion—$12 billion per year.[2] Studies of the US postal system also demonstrate that not only have prices gone up, but quality of service has declined. Between 1967 and 1987, mail delivery became 15% slower.[3]

In the US, there have been a number of postal reorganisations that have had mixed impacts. The reasons that these reorganisations have not been universally successful are that none of them have actually unleashed the forces of competition, and led to the kinds of systemic internal changes that we have referred to above. It is the absence of the competitive impulse that meant increasing costs simply translated to increasing prices. The lack of competition also created a risk averse mentality at all levels of the workforce, leading to much less innovation. The rewards of innovative activity do not flow to the business that is not facing the white heat of competition. One source of problems for the US Postal Services (USPS) has been the manner of regulation. In particular, the fact that the USPS must seek approval from the Postal Rate Commission for any innovative activity can have a significant dampening effect on innovation.

Costs in Private Firms

There is strong evidence that there is upward pressure on costs in SOEs, leading to higher prices, unless some form of subvention or subsidy is applied. Unlike in private companies, there is no shareholder discipline nor is there the profit-maximising drive as a method of increasing efficiency. The twin threat of bankruptcy or takeover that changes the behaviour of a private firm simply does not exist in the case of a SOE.[4] Data in the US suggests that the monopoly itself accounts for $2.5 billion in excess costs to mailers in the third-class bulk regular mail service.[5]

Many people have considered what privatisation of postal services might look like, and how the organisation can continue to fulfil its objectives in a commercial setting, subject to the rules that affect all businesses.

A number of different areas have caused most difficulty in the privatisation process as it has rolled out.

We will return to the discussions around the Japanese Postal Privatization as an example to see how the relevant issues play out in a real case. We will focus on the key areas which have proved problematic in the other liberalisation processes:

1   Anti-competition cross-subsidisation.
2   The use of the universal service subsidy to artificially reduce cost, thus making cross-subsidisation easier.
3   Non-transparent accounting mechanism leading to difficulties in detecting cross-subsidies.
4   Use of an artificially large reserved area to make it difficult for competitors to compete.

Naturally, many of these areas overlap, and so it is not possible to look at each in isolation. We will start with the Japanese approach to universal service. This is important because universal service was a major issue as the proposed privatisation went through the Japanese Diet. Japanese legislators were concerned with how the privatisation would affect rural service that a 2 trillion Yen universal service fund was required in order to allow the privatisation to actually happen. While the postal privatisation in the end did not go ahead in Japan in the end, the discussion around the privatisation is instructive.

Reserved Sector Analysis

The reserved sector is the sector that is reserved by statute for the government monopoly. It may be reserved by a cost, or more commonly a weight limit. Some countries will say that any mail below a certain weight cannot be sent by private operators.

Too large a reservation could have a very negative impact on competition in the market. Typically, postal companies reserve as part of their postal monopoly all goods up to a certain weight limit. This weight limit varies considerably around the world (among postal agencies). Recent European directives set the reservation at 100 g, declining to 30 g over time. A reservation that is significantly more than this will have competitive impacts for other market participants who could practice services in the reserved area.

There is a market impact of such reservations. These reservations can lead to the following effects:

1   Where there is competition between the postal company and other providers of non-postal services. The reservation prevents the non-postal service providers from functioning in the market at all. If the reservation is higher than it needs to be to meet a regulatory goal, then it will lead to market distortions in other related markets. There needs to be very close attention paid to the precise weight limit applied. This is because too high a weight limit unduly limits the ability of competitors to compete in the non-reserved sector and therefore limits competition. We believe that the appropriate weight limit for the reserved sector should be a maximum of 50 g progressively reduced over time. The reserved sector should also take into account other factors besides just weight, such as value.

2   The fact that there is a reservation enables the postal company to lower its costs in the non-reserved sector. This can distort the market for provision of services in the non-reserved sector. Essentially this can create a fund from which the Postal company can draw to engage in below-cost pricing in competitive market segments.

The European Commission has studied the weight and price limits of the reserved area in the postal sector (the "Study").[6] The DG XIII (now DG Infosoc) study found that even in countries with lower weight and price limits than the Directive 97/67/EC (which has now been superseded), the incumbent provider still had an "overwhelmingly strong market position." At the time (1998) the Postal Directive referred to a 350 g weight limit. The study found that a weight limit reduction to 100 g would nonetheless preserve 93% of the volume, and 85% of the revenues in the reservable area. Even a 50 g weight limit would keep 85% of volume and 77% of the reserved revenue. The impact on profitability of even the most adversely affected operator would be 6.5%.[7] The countries analysed did not indicate that a smaller reserved area induced massive new entry. In particular, Germany had fixed a reserved area of 50 g in 1998. The Swedish market is completely open (from 1993), yet Sweden Post's market share in the later marker is 96%.[8] Interestingly in Sweden small competitors did offer local post service (this also occurred in New Zealand). In Spain which was a completely liberalised setting with no reservation (and had been so since the 1960s), the competitors' market share was only 25% of the mail market. The study notes:

"The market entry of start-up small businesses is supposed to be very likely because starting to run a local postal business does not require large investment."[9]

Universal Service Issues

Universal service is a particularly difficult issue in the context of postal reform. Universal service is the requirement on postal companies to satisfy every customer even those in rural and remote areas. Naturally connecting customers in far flung areas is more costly than serving high density urban centres. The notion of universal service in postal is to ensure that as the market is reformed or liberalised new entrants do not simply serve the most profitable routes—leaving the incumbent to incur the high costs of serving the less profitable routes. The most common way of dealing with this issue (as in the telecom cases highlighted earlier) is to create a fund that the incumbent can dip into in order to satisfy the universal service obligation.

This looks like a very positive thing. Few can criticise the notion that serving people in remote areas is a good thing. However, often the next important question is never asked. The question of course is whether the fund is tailored to the regulatory goal that is being pursued, or whether it is more than this and hence could be misused.

Japanese Postal Privatisation Example

Throughout this chapter, we will use examples from the Japanese Postal privatisation. We have already discussed this in the context of financial services, given that rather unusually Japan Post contains within it the largest retail bank and the largest insurer in the world. However, of course Japan Post's core business is the letter mail monopoly, and so we turn to the effects of the privatisation on this, its core business.

Japanese Cabinet Decision on Basic Policy on Postal Privatisation (September 10, 2004) (the "Cabinet Decision") states that "Preferential measures shall be established if necessary to maintain universal service." This statement presents a number of problems as our studies of the universal service concept in a number of different areas demonstrates. The universal service commitment may actually lead to cost advantages for the incumbent that is subject to universal service obligations. This is because the universal service obligation means that the Post has a built-in infrastructure that can be used to lower costs for the provision of certain services outside the reserved sector. For example, the Post can use its infrastructure to lower the costs associated with sending packages through express mail, if it has an express mail arm. Instead of having to pay costs of C for utilisation of infrastructure which the private competitor must build out, the Post must pay only C-X (the cost of elements that are needed but have already been built out under the universal service obligation). This reduction of costs means that the Postal Company is at a cost advantage over the private competitor.

The universal service obligation therefore becomes more like a State Aid to use the language of European competition law. Applying the concepts that are applicable under European State Aid law, the universal service obligation becomes a governmental benefit that alters the cost base of the Post. Under European terms, the aid is an "economic advantage which it would not have obtained under normal market conditions." Under European law there is an exemption for services of general economic interest. However, cases have interpreted how the state aids rules apply.[10] In the case, the court ruled that in order for a benefit to be classifiable as a state aid, it must be capable of being regarded as an "advantage" conferred on the recipient undertaking which that undertaking would not have obtained under normal market conditions.

Four conditions (the so-called Altmark conditions) would have to apply in order for a state financial measure to escape classification as a state aid, incompatible with the common market, if it is for services to a recipient to discharge public service obligations. First, the recipient undertaking must actually have public service obligations to discharge and those obligations must be clearly defined. Second, the parameters on the basis of which compensation is calculated must be established in advance in an objective and transparent manner. Third, the compensation cannot exceed what is necessary to cover all or part of the costs incurred in the discharge of the public service obligations, taking into account the relevant receipts and a reasonable profit. Fourth, where the undertaking is not chosen in a public procurement, the level of compensation must be determined by a comparison with an analysis of the costs which a typical transport undertaking would incur (taking into account the receipts and a reasonable profit from discharging the obligations). In other words, any USO that exceeds this level would be a state aid under the Altmark test.[11] This would mean that any USO Fund which is based on a tax that competitors of the postal company would pay would almost automatically violate the Altmark principles because a fixed tax rate would be contingent on the variable of the revenues of the companies from which it is accrued, and that would have nothing to do with the actual cost of providing the universal service.

The allocation of such funds would, under European law, also constitute special and exclusive rights under Article 87 of the Treaty on European Union (TEU). In ascertaining whether the services are in the general economic interest, it is necessary to ask whether the service has special characteristics that distinguish it from other economic activities, and the transfer of funds must be shown to be connected to that specific characteristic. One of the relevant factors is a financial advantage beyond the cost of covering the USO being given to one of the undertakings. Hence, in order for a USO fund not to be caught under these provisions, it would need to be clearly defined.

We should note that there is an overlap between the universal service fund the reserved area. The reserved area itself contributes to the universal service obligation by giving a monopoly to the incumbent postal company. In this context, a valid question in determining the reserved area is what is the largest item that is considered essential for remote customers to send and receive (clearly this would not apply to send large packages sent overnight). It is also relevant that, for at least some customers, they are remotely located through choice. It should also be remembered that, as in telecom, some part of the universal service obligation is met by a growing postal market[12] (especially one where new entrants can flourish). Similar questions arise with respect to quality. What is the minimum quality which is tied to an *obligation* as opposed to a mere desire? We would all like our mail to be received the next day, but how much of that is strictly necessary? These are important questions that are often not asked in the context of universal service funds.

Even if a political decision is taken to impose a USO and obtain monies for that obligation from other parties, this has to be carefully handled in order to make sure that the incumbent company does not hide behind the USO as a way to engage in more anti-competitive practices. This has been dealt with in numerous ways across multiple network industry sectors. In general, a number of themes emerge:

1   The USO has certain benefits and certain costs. The costs and the benefits must be weighed against each other. The historical USO in the case of the Post Office will be an advantage as it has enabled the Post Office to build out the necessary infrastructure in rural and remote areas in Japan.
2   The USO should be supported by those who benefit from it. Clearly, people in the rural areas themselves benefit from the Universal Service Fund. However, equally clearly, people in rural areas cannot be expected to support the Universal Service fund entirely on their own. The obligation should therefore rest with taxpayers more generally.
3   Universal Service Fund obligations should not be imposed generally on competitors or potential entrants to market. This is because this damages competitive markets. These public sector restraints are effectively state aids to the Post Office which may be used to help it compete against other new entrants in sectors that are broadly competitive.

Anti-Competitive Cross-Subsidisation

The third major area which poses problems is the area of anti-competitive cross-subsidisation. This is similar to the issue we described in the telecom chapter. The fact that there is a reserved sector enables the incumbent postal company to use this monopoly to support low pricing in the competitive markets. If this pricing is below some measure of cost, then we may have anti-competitive cross-subsidisation. We will discuss this issue in greater detail in the chapter after we have discussed the market in which modern postal companies find themselves. We will also make some observations about the importance of competition agencies advocating pro-competition regulatory solutions in all these areas. Many of the issues were discussed in the EC v Deutsche Post (DP) case in which the funds paid to Deutsche Post under an illegal anti-competitive cross-subsidisation had to be disgorged by Deutsche Post.[13]

Importance of Competition Agency Engaging in Its Advocacy Role

It is imperative that the competition agency fully engage with other government agencies in its advocacy role. We have seen from the work of the International Competition Network (ICN) that it is very difficult for competition agencies to do this successfully, and early engagement is vital to the process. Where agencies wait until after the regulatory framework of a privatisation for example has already been established, it becomes very difficult to actually impact that regulatory structure in a pro-competitive fashion. In the ICN meeting in Bonn in 2005, many of the participants in discussing the role of competition advocacy noted that the key was to advocate early. The reason this was specifically mentioned was that there are many examples where a failure to advocate early has resulted in an inability to effectively make the case for competition after the regulatory structure and all that it implies has been concluded. Applying this in the Japanese context, if the competition agency does not react prior to the completed process of postal privatisation, assuming this happens, then it will find it extremely difficult to change the behaviour of the postal company itself, post-privatisation. There are many examples in the case of telecoms where there is a lot of data on privatisations where competition has not been successfully introduced into the privatisation programme.

The reason this is so fundamentally important is that frequently regulation and competition are conflicting policies. Regulation is a centrally planned process. However, competition relies upon decisions taken independently at the company level. The competition agency is the sole guardian of competition and consumers. It must operate to ensure that the voice of consumers is heard throughout the privatisation process. This means that the voice of the competition agency must be heard early in the privatisation process.

Just as in other areas, postal reform must be used in the context of the changing environment of the delivery of information generally. Just as in telecoms, and some of the other sectors we have looked at, there is a new communications economy that has changed the fundamentally the market in which postal firms find themselves. The new communications economy is described in the next section.

New Communications Economy

The manner in which information is delivered to consumers in the 21st century has completely changed from the manner in which it was delivered in the 20th. People are organising themselves around information and content, and less on materials and delivery. In this age, downward pressure on delivery costs brought about by the costless delivery of information over the internet and e-mail is almost total. This has caused a shift to the actual content—a complete reversal from the earlier situation where carriage was all important. It is hard to explain the full impact of information revolution. Suffice it to say that costs reductions brought about by the printing press were of the order of 1,000. Costs reductions brought about as a result of the invention of the microprocessor has dropped 10 million fold. The printing press led to the industrial revolution as the microprocessor has led to the information revolution.

In many ways, there is a new communications economy which applies to the way that all manner of products is transported across borders. In this new communications economy, the activities of a telecommunications provider, carrying information across the e-mail, or a mail carrier carrying the same information in documentary form, or an express delivery provider carrying the same document compete. Since these different platforms in some senses compete against each other, it is important that nothing is done that damages one or the other in the government's regulatory supervision of the sector. Economists have described the theory that underpins such competition the theory of monopolistic competition. Under this theory, individual monopolies can compete better against each other and promote overall consumer welfare in an economic sense, where the actual product market is much greater than the "monopoly" platform itself.

In the virtual world, the meaning of geography is also changing. People no longer think of themselves as creatures of a particular physical space. They are as likely to have interests in common with a social media group member in the US or Europe as in their home town of Tokyo. Equally, they may not have much in common with the nearest neighbours in the traditional sense of the word. Increasingly, connectivity is between people, and place is less relevant, just as content and not carriage is king.

Another thing that has changed is the speed with which global business is now conducted, powered by the internet. The speed of this change is so fast that the communications channels must be fast also.

All of this has important consequences for postal companies. Certainly, the current regulatory system which applies to the US Postal Service for example is not tenable, where even a postal increase takes 10 months to be approved. More significantly, it has implications for the cost structure of the postal market and its participants.

Public Goods Theory

The original motivation for a letter mail monopoly was that communications were a vital part of ensuring national identity. The Post satisfied the public goods theory, because consumers that benefited from the service did not deprive others of its benefits or limit supply. Under ordinary public goods theory, there is an incentive for a monopoly to be declared because of the market failure brought about as a result of the fact that we are dealing with public goods. Market failure occurs because the marginal cost curve of these kinds of public goods decreases to zero (instead of being a U-shaped curve as is the case with other goods). This occurs because they generally have very high fixed costs, such as infrastructure and so forth that means that the average cost curve declines. This means that as more and more services are provided, costs decline to zero as does price. This prevents the service provider from functioning and hence explains the request for state subvention or in extreme cases, state-mandated monopoly.

However, with the advent of things like e-mail, the internet, and telecommunications services, the arguments favouring public goods models are less and less persuasive. There is no longer a compelling public interest in ensuring that people have access to postal service because of the many other ways that information is transmitted. Furthermore, even if those arguments held up, there would be no reason not to permit competition, rather competition with regulated rates would be the norm in cases which are supposedly natural monopolies.

Conventional public goods analysis is frequently given as the reason supporting a natural monopoly. In this world, competition is shunned for fear that it will give rise to duplicated networks and less rather than more efficiency. In this context, it is important to note that legislated monopolies were created before the development of public goods theories. In other words, much of the economics to justify natural monopoly theory occurred well after the political forces that gave rise to natural monopoly did. The reality is that natural monopoly theories never did hold much weight. Viewing the competitive process as a dynamic one, we can see that few industries could say that the free market, applying a natural monopoly would allow consolidation to monopoly without the potential for new entrants or future competition acting as a restraint. Even if there are still adherents to the concept of natural monopoly, the number of industries that do not know have substantial infrastructural bypass capabilities is small and declining. One can look at the impact of wireless technology on the wired market and the arguments for natural monopoly there that were based on the high fixed costs of building the network. In the case of postal, this is even further removed from the realm of natural monopoly because of the ways that competing methods of getting information to people do not rely on or in any sense interconnect with the Post's network.

In the case of Japan, the fact JPN is the biggest bank and insurance company in the world is a useful prop for JPN when it is carrying out mail delivery functions.

A major issue is the notion of whether in a dynamic competitive environment, there is such a thing as excessive competition. "Ruinous" or "excessive" competition frequently harms high-cost producers and benefits consumers. Consumers are only harmed if the low-cost producers are actually producing below cost, and hence setting up the conditions for monopoly later. The whole concept of public goods theory rests on the presumption that in certain cases monopoly is the preferred market condition, because competition would invariably be excessive and lead to duplication. However, there is no reason in a public goods context why free competition as opposed to a legislatively granted monopoly might not lead to a large provider, and there is no inconsistency with normal competitive conditions that this should occur. It certainly does not mean that certain industries are prone to natural monopoly, or that the market fails in certain cases.

Even during the high-water mark of public goods theory or public utility theory, economists did point out that state privileges granted to state monopolies led to corruption and higher prices.

In most network industries that had previously been thought to be natural monopolies, such as the electric utilities industry, competition has been an important element in keeping downward pressure on price.

While the notion of natural monopoly in general has broken down, postal services are the least likely entities to qualify for such treatment. In electricity, telecom or gas facilities, one can see the very high fixed capital costs of building out complex wire or pipe networks. We do not see such high fixed costs for postal services. Because these fixed costs are not so high, the risk of future entry by other businesses would be high in a freely competitive scenario. This fact means that if the Post was privatised, then any tendency towards monopoly would be restrained by the possibility of future entry, thus obviating the need for excessive price controls.

Data suggests that lower cost transactions, that is, those that take longer to deliver will tend to lead to less vertical integration, whereas higher cost transactions lead to more integration. This is because of the shape of the curve of cost versus time to destination.

Since the Post tends to dominate the low speed/low-cost end of the market, there is even less of reason for a state-granted monopoly.

From a pro-poor standpoint, the letter mail monopoly acts to set a price floor in terms of delivery—deregulation might actually lead to more choice and lower prices.

The notion that the Post is somehow to be equated with very intensive capital cost industries such as electricity, telecommunications and gas is misleading. The industry is closer to trucking or airlines, where a large percentage of the costs is actually labour cost, as well as any legacy labour costs. Neither of these industries sink much capital into a network. In the case of postal in the US, labour costs are 80% of the total costs.[14] In the comparable industries of airlines and trucking, deregulation has taken place and has led to dramatic changes in pricing and cost structures. The postal company does have to contend with inflated labour costs (at least in the US) and a large amount of political power derived from the size of the labour force. Breaking up the Post into a number of players might actually lead to benefits arising from a reduction in the size of the labour force. Other ways of reducing costs include access pricing. Access pricing comes into play when it is possible for other companies to share the workload of the Post, thus reducing the Post's costs, and getting a better rate as a result. This would include, for example, where a company delivers mail to a central post office, thus eliminating one leg of the journey that the Post would have to engage in to lower costs. Discounts can also be applied for large pre-sort mailers in the case of the USPS. However, from the perspective of postal services, the more options are given to lower access charges, the greater the problem of stranded costs, as certain dedicated assets are left unutilised for greater periods.

Future mail delivery is a platform that admittedly now competes with other ways of sending out information, or, for example, paying bills. There are advantages to conventional snail mail, above e-mail such as privacy and identity theft concerns. It is likely in the future that postal bill paying may be competitive with e-bill paying. The important thing in terms of delivery of benefits to consumers is that these platforms are able to compete well against each other, following the theory of monopolistic competition.

Privatisation Options Through the Competition Lens

We have established that one of the major purposes behind privatisation is to unleash the forces of competition and generate the efficiency and management gains for the benefit of consumers of the service. One of the challenges that is typically faced by the Post is that it has very high labour costs, brought about by a high level of powerful public sector unions. Employee ownership therefore may be a way of minimising labour concerns, while at the same time ensuring that the conditions for privatisation result in a more productive workforce.

It will be important in any contemplated privatisation to ensure that the newly privatised Post cannot continue to engage in anti-competitive practices. These include the following:

1   *Deterring entry of new competitors.*
2   *Use of legacy privileges to secure a better competitive position.* Antitrust agencies should look for special tax breaks, customs privileges, even things like parking privileges that have an impact on the overall cost base.
3   *Predatory or exclusionary practices.* Agencies will have to be sensitive to the possibility that post services may elect to charge for certain services below cost to knock out competitors in certain areas, using the legally mandated monopoly in other areas to do so.

Many of these problems are solved by a series of regional postal companies. Such a divestiture also helps the issue related to labour changes, because it will deconcentrate the power of labour unions, and thereby allow the downward pressure on labour costs that competition brings to be effective.

The Japan Privatization law does contemplate a separation between the various lines of business of Japan Post although not on a regional basis. This is very important, and it is good that separation of these revenue streams is in the law. It will be important to ensure no possibility of cross subsidisation, so in implementing regulations, it would be important to see safeguards against this. De jure and de facto separation, including having separate price caps, if price caps are contemplated. Rigid accounting separation between these entities would also be required.

The Postal Privatization Commission does not currently have within its number representatives of the Competition Agency. This would be an important step in ensuring that pro-competitive concerns are addressed in the privatisation process itself. There are also special exemptions that are contemplated in the privatisation during the preparatory period for Japan Post. These include the ability of Japan Post to provide financing for international cargo transport. There are provisions that provide that this must be approved by the Privatization Commission, and that this activity must not unfairly harm those who provide like activities. This needs to be more clearly spelled out in the implementing regulations and the Competition Agency needs to be involved more closely in this area. A consumer welfare orientated approach, as opposed to the quasi-trade test that appears to be applied in the Japanese law needs elaboration. Where the law refers to the fact that the new postal companies will not do anything to damage the interests of companies that provide like services, the competition agency needs to weigh in with its views regarding precisely what this means in a competition context.

There are other areas such as insurance and financial services where the provisions are to ensure that the competitive relationships with other providers are not adversely affected. This is slightly clearer language, but it is important to ensure that the JFTC's views are actively sought in the crafting of the implementing regulations. We will come back to this issue in the context of financial services

The key areas where some competition safeguards are mandated are as follows:

1   Use of the USO as a shield for anti-competitive practices. Frequently, as noted earlier, the USO is so used.
2   A rigorous accounting separation mechanism among the various businesses is required to ensure that any anti-competitive cross-subsidisation is limited. In considering the costs for provision of a service, we recommend using a hypothetical private firm, and adding to that cost base the benefits accrued from being government owned, including all exemptions from taxes, licenses or any other regulatory process that private firms would have to engage in. All these costs should be added to the hypothetical benchmark. If the Post is charging below these costs, then a case can be made for anti-competitive cross-subsidisation.

Competition Issues in Japanese Privatisation That May Impact Trade Built-Out Infrastructure

It is clear that Japan Postal Company (one of the companies that will exist after the privatisation separates the postal company from the financial services and insurance arms of Japan Post) (JPCo) has benefited from having already built out its infrastructure. JPCo clearly will benefit from this legacy governmental ownership. There are a number of domestic express companies, such as Yamato and others that might be interested in providing postal services. The problem for them would be that they would have to compete against the much lower cost, already built-out infrastructure of JPCo. JFTC would have to develop a methodology to deal with this cost differential, by assigning a hypothetical benchmark cost for provision of postal service, and by developing accurate ways of evaluating the cost of the individual network elements.

In studies of the cost of the universal service obligation, a common theme emerges. The USO has both cost and benefit characteristics. Most studies conclude that any cost characteristics are outweighed by the benefit characteristics, and any cost savings by limiting the USO are dwarfed by savings from, for example, reducing the premium wage of government postal employees, who tend to be paid significantly more than private sector counterparts in comparable jobs. This is borne out even by a study authored by a number of Postal Rate Commission members.[15] In the Cohen et al. study, the authors note that the USO does not necessarily mean ubiquitous counter service. There are many ways of delivering the counter service, including providing mobile counters by postal couriers on their rounds (especially effective on rural routes). It noted that in the US, there were 38,000 postal facilities, many of which sat idle for large parts of the day. Closing some 7,000 of these would only give a saving of the order of 0.6% of total costs. Cost savings could also be incurred by reducing the delivery days on non-business routes (a 5-day service which is the norm in many countries would give rise to a 3% cost saving). The biggest saving by far however would be from equalising postal workers with comparable private sector counterpart wage levels. In the US, where postal worker wage levels are 21–35% higher than comparable private sector workers, the saving would be between 12 and 20% of total costs. The reason the wage premium is sustainable is the lack of competition, so once competition is introduced the Post Office would likely benefit from these major savings quickly. In most privatisations, substantial workforce reductions occur (40% between 1988 and 2001 in New Zealand, 15% between 2002 and 2005 in the UK). These reductions and costs savings dwarf tinkering with the USO. However, the significant benefit of the USO is the fact that as a result of it, the Post Office already has built out infrastructure.

The USO is often regarded as a set of obligations fixed in stone. We would argue that this is not the correct way of analysing the USO. The USO is a living obligation which may change with time and with liberalisation. For example, the notion of the USO requiring a certain number of counters, if technology supersedes the use of counters for sorting must itself be altered to take into account these dynamic changes.

As the population becomes more dense, so the Post Office benefits from economies of scope and economies of density. It has been shown that as the number of delivery points increases, the number of letter-carriers does not increase (because the same letter-carrier can easily service those increasing areas). Hence, the USO does not lead to costs rising with delivery points, since the bulk of the costs are in the letter-carrier itself. Yet Post Offices often argue that increasing volumes mean increasing USO costs. This example shows that USO cost, far from being proportional to increasing volumes, may actually be inversely proportional to volumes depending on the precise spread of the delivery points.

Auctioning Off Reserved Sector?

One method of stimulating competition in postal would be to auction the reserved sector, as one auctions spectrum in the telecommunications world. The problem with this approach is that it is not clear who would actually make competitive bids, especially since there would have to be an obligation to service the less profitable markets as a condition of the auction.

Economists have considered the potential for franchise bidding particularly in rural regions. As early as 1968, Demsetz wrote about the concept of franchise bidding, but the concept dates from the 19th century.[16] Franchise bidding requires the following: (i) Low sunk costs—many network utilities do not lend themselves to franchising because their sunk costs are very high, however, the advantage in the postal sector is that sunk costs are modest; and (ii) severability of network elements regional separation applies in the case of post or rail. Postal monopoly franchises could be awarded in different regions. The idea would be that these franchisees would have a franchise or franchisee relationship with the Postal incumbent. Such a relationship would require monitoring for quality standards as would be the case with any franchise relationship. However, commentators have expressed the concern that there are significant transaction costs associated with franchise bidding which may make it less attractive.

Mail delivery does lend itself to these kinds of franchise arrangements. It is useful to describe exactly how mail is collected, sorted and delivered. Mail is generally received from customers at multiple points. It is then transferred to a node, and sorted. It is then transferred to another node where it is re-sorted for onward delivery to specific customers. The service lends itself to competition because (a) there are very low levels of sunk costs (unlike other network industries), and (b) quality is easily observable—delivery times can be easily monitored. Transport capacity can also be leased in small portions without appreciable cost disadvantages. Postal operators have also not been responsible for built out infrastructure in the transportation area. Postal operators use roads and airways that already exist, and so the transportation cost is limited to vehicles (unlike in gas, telecom or electricity, where there are substantial sunk costs). Under franchise bidding, the inward and outward sorting of mail would be retained by the incumbent JPCo. JPCo would be subject to price regulation in this area. The transportation of mail between the nodes would be subject to competition. The transportation of unsorted mail to and from the nodes would be part of the franchise bid. The successful bidder would win both the collection from and delivery to a certain region, thus enabling monopolies of scope to be leveraged. The franchise bid would only apply in rural areas, so that the incumbent would continue to serve urban areas.

Interconnection

Another idea has been suggested in the case of Japan and other countries, in order to make the postal sector more competitive. The idea is that there should be interconnection between the new entrants into the network of JPCo. This would avoid the inefficient duplication of already built out infrastructure. Again, this is an interesting notion, but the problem would be the interconnection fee. If the Post is able to charge a prohibitively high interconnection fee, then we would simply replicate problems we have seen in the telecoms area. A number of cases in the telecoms area, such as Telmex (already discussed in previous papers), have shown us that excessive interconnection fees are very difficult to control when the incumbent has access to bottleneck facilities. The difference in postal arises from the question of how difficult it is to build postal infrastructure. Since much of the postal cost is in labour costs, and the facilities needed are not complex, it may be possible to build out infrastructure and that this infrastructure would not be unnecessarily duplicative. This would be analogous to having a number of express delivery pick-up facilities. This kind of infrastructure is to be differentiated from other networks where fixed capital cost is substantially greater, such as telecommunications, or electricity. While no-one considers it odd that there are a number of different express delivery pick-up facilities, it would be very strange to have multiple electricity grids (although even this area no longer exhibits the natural monopoly characteristics that it once did, due to competition from other sources of energy, and new technologies).

Weighed against this is the concern that interconnection with JPCo will be a one-sided negotiation with all the power in the hands of the Post. This is likely, if past experience is anything to go by to lead to a very high interconnection rate. It is unlikely that JFTC would be able to successfully discipline such a powerful actor, and this could lead to adverse market effects. In particular, a delay in being able to correct anti-competitive practices can have significant market effects for the new entrants in this market.

A significant difference between telecom interconnection and postal interconnection is that while postal interconnection can be limited, it cannot be denied totally, as there is nothing to stop users sorting and using the postal network in a bulk fashion, albeit at single piece rates. The question is what is the most efficient form of sanctioned access, and how should it work. One can have interconnection into upstream facilities, such as the mail-sorting equipment or downstream at delivery points. In the case of upstream, interconnection theories usually rely on some variant of the essential facilities doctrine. In the case of postal, these facilities are not truly essential in the antitrust sense. They can be duplicated with relative ease (or improved with innovation) and to require interconnection may not give rise to the most competitive solution in the long run. Given that the facility is not truly essential, normal competition rules should apply. If the Post Office increases the price, the new entrant may well develop its own solution, thus restraining the Post's pricing. However, this does not take into account the economies of scope and historic government ownership of the Post Office.

Downstream access would allow new entrants to deliver on some mail routes. The problem here is how to avoid cream skimming where new entrants simply leave the Post with all the high-cost routes.

In the UK, the postal reforms that applied to Royal Mail in 2006 involved licensed operators interconnecting into the Royal Mail's existing distribution system. In the UK, Britain's postal system was be fully liberalised from January 1, 2006. Under the postal reform in the UK, licensed companies have been able to collect, transport, and deliver letters and charge customers. Royal Mail and the Postal Company have been separated, and Royal Mail has been floated on the UK stock market.

Treatment of Costs in Alleged Cross-Subsidisation Cases

All businesses cross-subsidise. Not all of this activity is harmful to consumers. Indeed, many forms of cross subsidisation are beneficial to consumers. Cross-subsidisation is only harmful if it is anti-competitive. It is anti-competitive if it could lead to the elimination of competitors and then the increase in prices to supra competitive levels. One has to be extremely careful in ensuring that the discipline of competition is only used when behaviour is genuinely anti-competitive and leads to consumer harm. The ordinary test of what is anti-competitive behaviour is determined by an evaluation of whether the lower price (the price in the market which is being subsidised by the higher price in the non-competitive market) is indeed below some measure of cost (which is required in determining whether there is the potential for anti-competitive pricing in the future).[17] The theory is based on the fact that there can only be one reason for a price below cost, and that is to knock out competitors and recoup lost profit later.

The test for predatory pricing (Brooke Group) has to be modified in the case of cross-subsidisation by governmental entities or those that have legacy government ownership.[18] For companies that are government owned, the key issue is that because governments are not profit maximisers the element of the Brooke Group test that requires lost profits to be capable of being recouped is not as important. Governments are at best revenue maximisers (and even this is doubtful—see USPS sponsorship of US cycling team, even though they already have a letter mail monopoly). Therefore, if there is below cost pricing, we would argue that this is prima facie evidence of anti-competitive cross-subsidisation. Indeed, the EU cases on this issue assume anticompetitive cross-subsidisation by governments, even absent a possibility of recoupment of lost profit.[19] The question is "what is the impact of a pre-existing government ownership?"

We have discussed anti-competitive cross-subsidisation before in other cases, and much of what was discussed then holds true in this area as well. Just as in other areas, harmful cross-subsidisation arises where the lower price (the one that is being complained of) is below some measure of cost. The precise measure of cost is, of course, the key to ensuring that a state supported company does not have an undue and all-importantly consumer welfare destroying advantage. As in other cases that we have looked at, the nature of the governmental privileges and benefits need to be carefully examined to ascertain its actual impact on cost.

Impact of Pre-Existing Government Ownership

Measure of Cost

The usual measure of cost in determining competitive pricing is marginal cost. Marginal cost, being difficult to compute is usually proxied by average variable cost. The precise measure of cost used is absolutely key to the determination of whether there are anti-competitive practices or not. This will then drive the entire determination of whether there has been an anti-competitive practice or not.

In order to ensure that the market and related markets are kept competitive, it will be necessary to be extremely careful in the analysis of costs. The following factors must be borne in mind as we analyse costs.

1   *Shared infrastructure cost.* In the case of the Post, there are a number of shared costs, which can be attributed both to the letter mail monopoly infrastructure and to the parcel service. This issue of shared infrastructure cost was considered in the case of *Deutsche Post v. Commission*.[20] In that case, in looking at the costs of providing services, Deutsche Post (DP) argued that it needed the 33 freight centres that were used in the postal system to provide its parcel service. It therefore sought to include in the cost calculations the capital cost of setting up the freight centres. There is also some shared staffing between these two functions. It was also found in the DP case that some dedicated B-to-B parcels were delivered jointly with B-to-C parcels in standard delivery rounds. In other words, there were a number of areas where DP's express arm benefited from certain sunk cost items that it had as a result of its letter

mail system. Since that system was a monopoly, its express delivery arm had artificially lower costs than a hypothetical competitor would have. Hence these costs must be added to the stated cost of providing the service. In evaluating these issues for other postal companies, it will be necessary to ascertain how it conducts its parcel delivery arm, and whether it uses some of the letter mail infrastructure to perform these services. In the DP case, the mail-order service costs could be specifically attributed to the mail order function. There is also a question as to the cost of running the capital, maintenance, and supplies of the network, and how these costs should be apportioned between the postal and express arms.

2   *Historical legacy of government ownership.* It is necessary to track back to establish the real impact of the historical legacy of government ownership. There may be transfers of assets, real estate, or other property to the formerly state-owned company, perhaps even as part of the privatisation process. The British Post Office which intervened in the DP case, maintained that the transfer of any property to the public postal service constituted unlawful state aid. In the DP case, there were also transfers of funds from the DB-Telekom to DB-Postdienst which allegedly constituted state aid. In the case of other privatisations or liberalisations, a question will be whether there are any funds or property transfers which could constitute both anti-competitive aid, but also would lead to the reduction of the costs of providing the express delivery service. In Japan, as part of the privatisation process, the Universal Service Fund will be met from the proceeds of the sale of the constituent parts of the JPN. This is a very important area which needs to be carefully monitored by the JFTC. This is because these funds could be regarded as transfers as defined earlier. They could be problematic from a competition and market distortion standpoint. An assessment would also have to be made about any other funds that have been transferred to JPCo from other branches of JPN prior to, or as part of the privatisation.

3   *Historic costs associated with government ownership.* In the DP case, DP maintained that it had historic costs that private competitors did not have—these included above average wages, redundancy payments, government sponsored programmes such as affordable housing for its employees and so forth that together constituted an atypical cost element. *See id.* It is likely that other postal incumbents would make similar arguments to justify anti-competitive activity. It is important to note that many of these alleged atypical components are not really higher cost that private competitors would have, and to the extent they are usually dealt with in prior transfers of assets from State to the Post (as they were in the DP case).

4   *Targeted rebates.* DP gave rebates to major users. These rebates were
    partially funded out of its revenues from the letter mail monopoly, and
    from other revenues. One of the problems for DP was that it was clear
    from the documents that the rebate strategy was designed to deal with
    DP's declining market share and not to deal with any concept of a uni-
    versal service component.
5   *Legacy-based privileges and benefits.* JPN's legacy may mean that the
    JPCo has certain privileges and benefits that it has as part of its govern-
    ment status. These can include preferential tax status, parking privi-
    leges and preferential customs status when sending packages across
    national boundaries. These kinds of benefits must also be added to the
    cost of the provision of the service.
6   *Interaction between USO, reserved sector and costs of service provi-
    sion.* In the DP case, DP maintained that it had a USO for delivery of
    all postal parcels up to 20 kg. This is a very high weight limit. The
    notion of what the universal service function covers is naturally linked
    to what is covered by the Reserved Sector. The USO should only cover
    what truly constitutes essential mail—hence we advocate a 30 g target.
    Allowing the reserved sector size to increase will allow the USO to be
    used to defend anti-competitive activity and to lead to a calculation of
    costs attributed to provision of the express service that understates the
    actual costs. This will in turn make it much harder to demonstrate that
    pricing on the express sector is below some measure of cost.
7   *Prevention is better than cure.* In our experience, around the world,
    once an incumbent is allowed to engage in anti-competitive practices,
    it is very difficult to discipline the incumbent because of its significant
    political power. It is much better to ensure that the regulatory design
    precludes anti-competitive practices, and monies are not available to
    JPCo to engage in such behaviour. This is why it is important to limit
    the size of the reserved sector, to ensure that the postal sector is com-
    petitive as possible, and that opportunities for the exploitation of bot-
    tleneck facilities are very strictly limited.

Concluding Thoughts on Market Distortions in the Postal Sector

We have demonstrated by reference to the cases as well as the ongoing
Japanese postal privatisation that liberalisation can indeed lead to consumer
welfare-enhancing outcomes, but that the manner of the liberalisation or privatisation is key to determining how that process unfolds. There are many
hidden traps concealed in anti-competitive regulation that can forestall these

consumer welfare-enhancing outcomes. It is critical that competition agencies are allowed to have their say in the regulatory process, and that they do make explicit the consumer costs of a particular anti-competitive regulation. It is not, of course, for competition agencies to determine regulatory structure, but if the consumer costs of a regulatory structure are not made explicit, then legislators (and more importantly people) will not have the information they need to make good decisions. We will in the final chapter tie up the common, cross-cutting themes that seem to emerge from this treatment.

Notes

1 Edward L. Hudgins, *The Last Monopoly: Privatizing the Postal Service for the Information Age*, Cato Institute, 1996.
2 Robert W. Hahn and John A. Hird, The Costs and Benefits of Regulation; Review and Synthesis, 8 Yale J. Reg. 233, 264 (1990).
3 James Bovard, *The Last Dinosaur: The US Postal Service*, Policy Analysis No. 47, Cato Institute, 1985, ff.
4 *See* treatment of La Poste and Italian Postal state aids cases, *see* Commission Decision 2008/204/EC, 2008 O. J. (L 63/16); Commission Decision 2009/178/EC, 2009 O. J. (L64/4).
5 *See* Thomas M. Lenard, The Efficiency Costs of the Postal Monopoly: The Case of Third-Class Mail, 6 J. Reg. Econ. 421 (1994), ff.
6 European Commission, *Studies on the Impact of Liberalization in the Postal Sector: Study on the Weight and Price Limits of the Reserved Area in the Postal Sector*, Directorate General XIII, European Commission, 1998.
7 *Id.*, at 6.
8 *Id.*, at 17.
9 *Id.*, at 23.
10 *See* Case C-200/00, Altmark Trans GmbH and Regierungspraesidium Magdeburg v. Nahverkehrsgesellschaft Altmark GmbH, 2003 ECR I-7747.
11 Altmark case. Case 280-00, Judgement of 24 July, 2003.
12 European Commission, *The Impact on Universal Service of the Full Market Accomplishment of the Postal Internal Market in 2009—Final Report*, DG MARKT/2005/03/E, European Commission, 2006; ("Market forces will increasingly contribute to a more efficient universal service provision . . .").
13 CASE COMP/35.141-Deutsche Post AG of 20 March 2001.
14 *See* Edward L. Hudgins, *The Last Monopoly: Privatizing the Postal Service for the Information Age*, Cato Institute, 1996.
15 Robert Cohen et al., *The Cost of Universal Service in the US and Its Impact on Competition*, Proceedings of Wissenschaftliches Institut für Kommunikationsdienste GMBH, 17–19 November 2002.
16 Harold Demsetz, Why Regulate Utilities, 11 J. Law Econ. 55 (1968).
17 Brooke Group v. Brown & Williamson, 509 US 209 (1993).
18 Brooke Group Limnited v Brown and Williamson, 509 US 209 (1993).
19 Case C-202/07P, France Télécom SA v Commission of the European Communities, 2003 ECR I-2369.
20 Case T-421/07, Deutsche Post AG v. European Commission, 2008 ECR II-1233.

5   Conclusion

This short volume has looked at a number of areas of privatisation and how market distortions in these different areas meant that the benefits of privatisation were not as well realised as they could have been. Privatisation allows countries to open up particular sectors that were under government control to external firms. There is a link to the services liberalisation agenda, as opening through privatisation increases the ability of foreign service providers to access service markets in the privatising country. Our analysis of specific sectors highlights a number of common themes which emerge.

First, the purpose of privatisation is to allow the forces of competition to deliver better choice, lower prices and more efficiency for consumers. Where competition does not inform the regulatory design, or is forestalled, privatisation has tended to deliver a private monopoly without regulation.

We have seen that universal service commitments, public service obligations and so on can be used by incumbent entities to engage in anti-competitive cross-subsidisation between the regulated sector where they have a monopoly and other aspects of their business where competition is allowed. This can have a damaging impact on service delivery and consumers. This has been particular true for telecoms and postal sectors.

Interconnection into core assets which are necessary for the provision of services is also an area where lack of competition can lead to increased price and reduced services. We have seen that this is particularly important in the case of electricity and gas privatisation, where access to an essential core facility can become a competition blockage. Interconnection policies should therefore put a premium on their pro-competitive aspects.

There is also a lot of unfinished business resulting from privatisations which are often only the first step in introducing true competition into the particular sector concerned. It should be the ambition of a government engaged in privatisation to move from a framework governed by ex ante regulation to one government by ex post competition where possible. This

DOI: 10.4324/9781003360476-5

means there is a significant role for the interaction between the competition regulator and the sectoral regulator. Of course there are regulatory choices and requirements that must be met in order for the necessary services to be properly delivered, but these regulatory choices and satisfaction of requirement must be implemented in the most pro-competitive manner possible. It is here that a dialogue between the competition agency and the sectoral regulator can be particularly useful. The competition regulator is aware of different competition outcomes in different sectors and can readily apply learnings from other sectors which a sectoral regulator is too narrow to do. Similarly, there are very specific aspects of the sector being regulated which the competition agency may not have studied. It is only by bringing these two bodies of knowledge together that a better result can be obtained.

Privatisations are a way in one scenario where countries open themselves up to foreign (and domestic) service providers. The problems we have seen that prevent the benefits of privatisation from flowing through to consumers also illustrate the important role that Anti-Competitive Market Distortions play in this sphere. Governments who are serious about sustainable privatisation that delivers long term competitive benefits for consumers must ensure that competition on the merits is driven through the process.

Index

Printed in the United States
by Baker & Taylor Publisher Services